COOKING
DINNER

With
Eleanor
Goetz

SERENDIPITY PRESS
Wilmington, Delaware

Cooking Dinner
with Eleanor Goetz

The News-Journal Company, Wilmington, Delaware, has authorized the republication of some material appearing in this book. All of the artwork by Robert Laird and many of the recipes were originally printed in *The Morning News*.

Library of Congress catalog card number 79-67241

Printed in the United States of America

Design by Frank Coburn

To my family with love . . .

in alphabetical order

Nancy, Robert, Rush, Sarah and Steve

Acknowledgments

This collection has come from my own kitchen and the kitchens of family, friends and readers. For their kindness and generosity I want to thank a great many people beginning with Margaret Crabtree, my food page editor who helped edit this book, and to Bob Laird, my talented illustrator.

For their contribution of recipes great appreciation goes to Frances Lippincott, Marjorie Lauve, the late Anne Ferrara Hiller, Tunie Wright, Rita Tuttle, Martha Espedahl, Frani Beach, Dot Ward, Betty Hilliard, Pat Tabibian, Connie Metcalf, Joyce Robinson, Agnes Scott, Virginia Hanby, Martha Shelnutt, Jo De Luca, Suzanne Bush, Vivian Rash, Martha Rogers, Franz Portmann, The Hrab family, Georgette Cole, George Anna Theobald, Gloria Mark, Marge Clymer, Sophia Tarabicos and my sisters, Irene Tedrow and Alice Stephan.

Special thanks are in order to the Hotel DuPont and Winkler's Restaurant, both in Wilmington, and the Corner Cupboard Inn, Rehoboth.

A few recipes are reprinted from My Mother's Cookbook, published by Little Brown House, Harper's Ferry, West Virginia. Two of the commentaries, Contentious Cooks and Food Can Be Funny, were originally published in *Delaware Today* magazine and are reprinted with permission.

If I have omitted anyone, I can only ask forgiveness.

v

About the Author

Eleanor Goetz, unlike most authors of cookbooks, is a professional newspaper woman. Since 1976, her special field has been a weekly column on cooking for The Morning News, Wilmington, Delaware.

Born in McKeesport, Pennsylvania, she grew up in a home where fine Swedish cooking was a matter of course. Following graduation from the University of Pittsburgh, she embarked on an interesting and varied career which was to include retailing, advertising, public relations, television, music and show biz.

In the 1950's, under the name of Eleanor Glenn, she conducted a daily cooking show on Wilmington television. This was followed by a talk show on WPTZ-TV in Philadelphia. Her newspaper career began in 1968 with a weekly column "What a World" for The Morning News. Later she became a full time feature writer.

During all the years of communicating and writing, Mrs. Goetz traveled extensively throughout Great Britain, Europe, and the Caribbean. She has lived at one time or another in Australia, England and Germany, and in her travels, has been a passenger on 20 different ocean liners. This wide-ranging travel enriched her tastes and skills in cookery. Everything came together in 1976 when she returned to The Morning News after a year's residence in London and started her food column.

Mrs. Goetz has tested and published more than 1,200 recipes in her column. These are transmitted by Gannett News Service to the chain's 80 papers in the United States, Guam and the Virgin Islands.

Contents

Introduction

Years ago, my husband and I were privileged to enjoy a summer-long holiday in Europe with our two pre-teen children.

When we arrived home, my husband literally stood in the front hallway, put down the bags he was carrying, and without removing his coat, said to me in the kindest tone of voice, "You have now been out to dinner for sixty nights in a row. I'd rather not hear anything about going out for dinner for a long, long time."

The deep desire for the pleasure and stability of the family together at the evening meal has remained a constant in a world where social values are so topsy-turvy that one can scarcely cope with the changes. Even in the light of the rapidly altering roles of women, this daily responsibility has remained the common denominator of most of us.

Whether we go out to work, or stay home, whether we're well-heeled or struggling to survive, whether we're activists or tories, most of us have the responsibility of getting as good a dinner as we can on the table every evening.

That is what this book is all about. All the recipes can be accomplished by the average cook. There is no need for special equipment, or exotic or hard-to-find ingredients. From the 1500 or more recipes that have appeared on my food pages over the last three years, I have selected the ones my readers have enjoyed most, then added a number of new recipes, not published before, as far as I know.

These recipes have not been just tested—they have been used.

You will not find basic material like how to roast a rib, or fifteen pages on how to bake bread. This is rather a compendium of different ways to cook the vegetables you always cook, to stretch a pound of ground beef to feed your six, to meet the everyday problems of getting dinner just about every day for your family and for guests.

Sometimes these problems require more than cooking instructions, so in between recipes you will find some comments about survival in the kitchen, and at the table.

For many of you, consistently pleasant, congenial family dinners must seem as idealized as a Norman Rockwell magazine cover.

You may be blessed with a husband who's always late, or worse, uncommunicative. A teenager who eyes anything on his plate that isn't a hamburger with suspicion and outrage. "What's that?" he demands.

No matter what time dinner is scheduled, someone always needs to be driven somewhere at 7:00 P.M., and when Little League is in bloom, forget it. Nobody can plan dinner around that schedule.

Siblings flare up and leave the table. Fathers occasionally roar and rant, leaving the little ones wide-eyed and wondering. And in the wake of all this, you can get pretty snappish yourself as you watch the effort you put into dinner going down the drain.

Serenity. That's what is required, and that's so very hard for most of us to achieve.

In a newspaper feature earlier this year, a monk at a Zen Center was remarking about the excellent food served the center. "We don't let new people work in the kitchen. We believe you need experienced, calm people there. Good karma creates good food," he said.

The need for serenity in the kitchen is urgent. Without it, you read the recipe wrong, you cook badly, and end up cross at the dinner table.

Over the years, I have concluded that two things are basic—serenity and enough time. As the song says, you can't have one without the other.

When you are sore pressed for time, you lose your cool. That's when you spill the sugar on the floor, cut yourself and are impatient with the children. Even though you never achieve serenity, there are ways to make time work for you, and this is particularly vital for women who work full time.

If you have young children, it's pleasant to work quietly in the kitchen after they've gone to bed, not to do anything dramatic, but to start a good stew for tomorrow, or stick a box cake in the oven. If you're a morning person, get some preparation done before you go to work.

Many working women have turned to the crock pot, knowing happily all day that dinner is cooking away at home. I think this is fine some of the time, but day in and day out, crock pot cooking comes to a kind of sameness.

Your freezer is your very best time saver. Make one to eat and one to freeze. Then on that night when there is literally not the time to start from scratch, you hit the ice box for a good hot dinner.

One of the hardest things I had to learn in the kitchen was to take some advice from my Mother which would have saved me many discouraged moments. As a bride, I really resented every time she came into the kitchen when I was cooking and said, "You know it's easier if you clean up as you go along."

It took a long time for that to sink in, and in the meantime, there were many occasions when I stood in a kitchen with barely a square foot of counter space visible, with pans in the sink, and a general air of chaos over all. You get to feeling like Cinderella left at home as you look at the children playing outside, your husband sitting on the terrace with the paper.

In a sea of self-pity, you bang things around as you repair the mess, hoping someone will notice poor you.

If you think about it, it takes about twice as long to clean up general confusion as it does to—you know what my Mother said.

In the same moralistic vein, you may be pricked by this lapse—not making certain you have all the ingredients for a recipe before you start. Can there be anything worse than getting well into the thing and suddenly realizing that you don't have a can of tomato paste that's required? You can't change the menu—you're too far along. Out comes the car. In goes the baby, strapped in his car seat. You go to the market where you stand in line, so-called Express, for at least ten minutes, drive home, unstrap baby, get back to the kitchen, by now in a perfect snit.

Read the recipe twice, and check for all ingredients.

Last on the let's-be-serene list is a ludicrously obvious statement you might think about when you have time.

If something takes an hour to cook, you can't cook it in half an hour.

And a good karma to you.

Starters...

Appetizers and Hors d' Oeuvres

You protest? Your everyday dinner doesn't start with such folderols, only your parties?

Think again. When your husband comes home and sits down at the kitchen table to have a cold beer, he wants something to nibble. A piece of cheese, some crackers, a little something.

When you get home from work, as Robert Benchley once said, come out of the rain and into a dry martini, you want something with it— more olives, a little dish of nuts or the like.

The first course doesn't happen at the table as a rule, and since we're a nation of "nashers," you might find that your family would like to get off the potato chip kick and into some really good nashes.

In this area, your freezer is your trusty friend. Most hors d' oeuvre recipes make dozens, things like cheese biscuits, and cheese puffs, that can be frozen and always on the ready. That old reliable cream cheese turns into Boursin or pepper cheese in minutes—nice to have on hand.

While you will find some elegant starters in the pages ahead, you will also find family fare. The trick is to control the eating thereof. If I make a whole plate of stuffed eggs, my son will eat every one, like an automatic stoker, if not held firmly in control. Never put the bowl of macadamias beside a compulsive talker in your family. He will down them without even thinking—those little globes that are at present priced like emeralds.

The first course is the beginning, not an end to itself and should be light and pleasing, but stimulate rather than dull the appetite.

Many of the good things that go into first courses are expensive. Yet one of the best and most liked appetizers I make are little rounds of French bread, spread with a light coat of mayonnaise and topped with a paper thin slice of sweet onion. Try little rye rounds with a piece of sweet pimento and a bit of anchovy.

You can play around with the stuffed bread recipes you will find ahead. They freeze very well, can be sliced frozen, and thaw in minutes. Often you will discover you can utilize leftovers to add variety to their fillings.

By and large, Europeans are astounded at our serving their after dinner cheese before the meal. Things made with cheese, OK, but not wedges or slices.

All except the Dutch that is, who serve the most massive first course in the world. Guess when? At breakfast. The Dutch breakfast begins with an enormous platter of various cheeses and cold meats after which you get down to the serious business of bacon and eggs.

It's wonderful.

Stuffed Bread,
Variation on a Theme

This appealing appetizer is best made with the long very thin French loaf, but you can use the small loaves that come in a package of two, called French rolls, about six inches long. If you use brown and serve bread, bake it before starting to fill it.

Method I: Cut off the ends, and if you're using the rolls, cut in half horizontally; if bread, cut in 2 manageable lengths, and then cut across horizontally. Remove the center of the bread with a fork. Now you can stuff the top and the bottom with two different mixtures making a handsome slice for serving. Here is one suggestion:

Spread thickly inside the top, a mixture of

½ cup soft butter
½ cup minced parsley or water-
cress

some of the bread center,
crumbed
some finely chopped pimento

Fill the bottom, heaping up, with a mixture of

3 ounces soft cream cheese
3 ounces deviled ham
1 tablespoon mustard

1 teaspoon grated onion
few dashes of Tabasco

Press top and bottom together and chill thoroughly, wrapped up. Slice thinly to serve. This freezes very well. You will find you can slice it frozen, and it will thaw in minutes.

Method II: Cut off the ends of a French loaf and, with a fork, pull the center of the bread out leaving a sturdy wall about ¾ of an inch thick. Fill the cavity with a mixture of almost anything, starting with ground or processed cold cooked meat—chicken or ham work well. Add chopped dill pickles, finely chopped hard boiled eggs, herbs, chopped chives and enough mayonnaise to hold it together. The mixture should be very firm.

If you plan to freeze this, skip the hard boiled eggs and mayonnaise. Use a little cream cheese to hold it together.

Chill under wraps, slice thinly to serve.

APPETIZER CHEESE CAKE

A well assembled creation for your next cocktail party.

melted butter
2 cups finely crushed cheese
    crackers
2 cups sour cream
1 green pepper, finely minced
½ cup stuffed green olives,
    finely chopped
½ cup celery, finely chopped

2 tablespoons lemon juice
1 small onion, minced
1 teaspoon salt
1 teaspoon paprika
1 teaspoon Worcestershire
    sauce
dash of Tabasco

Line an 8 inch square or round pan with wax paper, leaving enough over the edges to bring up and cover the cheese cake.

Brush the bottom and sides with melted butter, then line the bottom of the pan with crushed crackers ½ inch thick. Put the sour cream in a bowl and stir in all other ingredients except the remaining crackers.

Spread a ½ inch thick layer of sour cream mixture over the crumbs in the pan, then fill the pan with alternate layers of crumbs and cream, ending with crackers.

Cover with the excess wax paper, and refrigerate for at least twenty four hours. To serve, turn out on a plate, remove paper and cut into small squares or wedges.

BOURSIN CHEESE

The real stuff has gotten so expensive that this make-at-home is invaluable. It tastes just like the real thing.

16 ounces cream cheese
8 ounces butter or margarine
2 crushed garlic cloves or 1
    tablespoon garlic powder

1 tablespoon oregano
¼ teaspoon each, thyme, basil,
    marjoram, dill
dash of salt and pepper

Combine herbs and rub through a sieve. Have cheese and butter at room temperature. Cream together and add all seasonings, blending well. Chill and serve with crackers, Melba toast or tiny slices of French bread.

CHEESE BISCUITS

They look like cookies but they're really hors d' oeuvres. Make them just bite size and prepare for compliments.

1 stick butter, softened
¼ pound Cheddar cheese,
    grated, or 1 jar sharp cheese
    spread (5 ounces)

1 cup flour
½ teaspoon salt
¼ teaspoon cayenne pepper
pecan halves

Blend all ingredients except nuts until smooth. Form into little balls, then press down with your thumb. Put a pecan half in each biscuit firmly so that it won't come off in the baking. Bake on ungreased cookie sheets until golden brown, 8 to 10 minutes at 400°F.

INA'S CHEESE COOKIES

Cheese cookies to go with drinks or salads are great to have on hand. These will keep nicely in a container with a lid or, if you prefer, freeze a bag full.

2 sticks soft margarine
2 cups grated sharp Cheddar cheese
2 cups flour

2 cups Rice Krispies
3 dashes of Tabasco
½ teaspoon salt

Mix everything together in a bowl. With the dough, form one inch balls, arrange on an ungreased baking sheet, then press each one down with a fork, making ridges and flattening. Bake at 350°F for 15 to 20 minutes, watching after 15 minutes for quick browning.

LITTLE CHEESE PUFFS

These are not only fun to make but irreplaceable as freezer goodies to keep on hand for sudden social exigencies. Let them drop in—you've got gougéres at the ready, to serve just heated, or quickly filled with ham or chicken or cream cheese and chutney.

¼ cup margarine
1 cup water
½ teaspoon salt
dash of white pepper

1 cup flour
4 eggs
1 cup grated Swiss cheese

Heat water, margarine, salt and pepper until the water boils and the margarine is melted. Add the flour all at once, beating the mixture vigorously. Suddenly, the mixture will leave the sides of the pan—at which point remove from the fire.

Add the eggs one at a time, beating well by hand after each addition until the mixture is smooth and shiny. Stir in the cheese, distributing evenly.

Now, using a teaspoon, drop little amounts of dough on lightly greased baking sheets. You should have about 36 puffs, which will give you an idea of the size. Bake at 375°F for 25 to 30 minutes, when the puffs will be golden. Because there will be a tiny bit of damp dough remaining inside, some folks remove the puffs from the oven, pierce each one and return to the oven to finish. This dries out the inside.

To freeze: Arrange uncovered on the cookie sheet and freeze until fairly firm, then put in Baggies for later use.

CHICKEN LIVER PÂTÉ

After trying many, many pâtés, I have realized, the simpler, the better. This recipe is very easy, but you want to use good brandy. A note of advice: if the sautéing onions give up a great deal of liquid, drain a little off before putting in the chicken livers. Do not double this recipe. Make it twice if necessary.

l pound chicken livers, halved   1 teaspoon salt
1 large Bermuda onion   fresh ground pepper
½ pound butter (not margarine)   ¼ cup brandy

Peel and chop the onion. Sauté in 4 tablespoons butter for about 5 minutes, stirring. Add 4 more tablespoons butter and cook the chicken livers until no pink remains. Season with salt and pepper. Warm the brandy and pour over the livers. Ignite and allow the flames to burn out.

Put the contents of the skillet into a processor, or half the contents in the blender, and process until smooth as possible. Repeat the process in the blender for the other half.

Put the liver purée through a fine sieve. Cream the remaining ¼ pound of butter until it is light, then mix it into the purée. Taste for seasoning and spoon into small crocks or soufflé dishes. Lay wax paper right on the surface to keep the air from it. Chill and serve with crackers or Melba toast.

CUCUMBER DIP

When the garden grows, the lure of fresh mint or dill makes this dip positively sing.

1 cup cucumber, seeded, chopped
2 cups thick yogurt
1 garlic clove, crushed

2 tablespoons olive oil
1 tablespoon fresh minced dill or mint
1 tablespoon lemon juice

Sprinkle salt over the chopped cucumber and let it stand for at least 15 minutes. Press dry with paper towels. Combine with the rest of the ingredients and chill. This makes 3 cups. Use as a dip for vegetables or, interestingly, as a topping for fresh cooked green vegetables.

KENNETT CONNECTIONS (MUSHROOMS)

Prize winner in a contest for original and desirable appetizers, this goodie was created by Gloria Mark.

24 perfect mushrooms, one inch diameter
1 package Boursin or Alouette cheese

3 tablespoons melted butter

Wipe the mushrooms with a damp paper towel. Remove the stems and, if necessary, scoop out a bit to make a roomy bowl. Roll the caps in the melted butter.

Fill each cap with cheese, heaping it slightly. Place the caps on a buttered baking sheet and cover loosely with aluminum foil. Bake in a 375°F oven for 5 to 7 minutes, then remove the foil and let the cheese puff and become dotted with golden brown spots. Serve right away.

MUSHROOMS WITH SPINACH SOUFFLÉ

The trick here is to buy small handsome mushrooms, all about the same size. After that this is a very easy and attractive appetizer.

1 box frozen spinach soufflé
20 small good looking mush-
    rooms
butter

salt
nutmeg
grated Parmesan cheese

Thaw the spinach soufflé until soft. Stem and clean the mushrooms and butter the outsides. In the bottom of each mushroom cavity, sprinkle a bit of salt and a grating of nutmeg.

Fill the mushrooms with soufflé and sprinkle a little Parmesan over each. Arrange on a baking sheet. Half an hour before serving time, place them in a 350°F oven and bake for 30 minutes.

PEPPED UP POPCORN

An inexpensive and habit forming appetizer for TV munching or an informal party.

Start with a great big bowl of popped corn. Melt a stick of butter in a skillet along with 2 cloves of garlic, peeled and halved. When the butter just begins to change color, sprinkle in 1 tablespoon of chives and 1 tablespoon of chopped parsley. Remove the garlic and toss the popcorn with the butter.

You see where this goes? That's just a sample. You can use basil and oregano if you're Italian, curry if you're Indian, dill butter if you're Scandinavian. The possibilities are mind bending.

Have fun!

IRENE'S OLIVE WHIRLIGIGS

Sister Irene serves these with the first drink, "before everybody has gotten up to go to the appetizer table."

1 cup shredded sharp Cheddar cheese
3 tablespoons softened butter
fresh ground pepper
½ cup sifted all purpose flour

½ cup chopped stuffed green olives
6 slices bacon, crisp fried, crumbled

In a bowl, blend the cheese, butter and pepper. Stir in the sifted flour to make a pastry. Roll between sheets of wax paper into a rectangle, 10 x 6 inches. It should be about ⅛ inch thick.

Sprinkle olives and bacon over the pastry, then roll like a jelly roll. Wrap well in the wax paper and chill for at least 1 hour.

Cut into quarter inch slices and arrange on an ungreased baking sheet, 2 inches apart. Bake at 400°F for 10 minutes. This should make 40 appetizers.

Why not do twenty at a time on two sheets? Then you can go around again with hot whirligigs.

TOASTED SWISS CANAPES

This makes a great many little rounds. You might want to cut the recipe in half for a smaller do.

2 cups grated Swiss cheese
8 slices bacon, fried crisp, crumbled
celery salt

onion juice
mayonnaise
rye bread rounds

Combine all ingredients adding just enough mayonnaise to hold together, celery salt and onion juice to taste. Spread on little rye rounds and bake on cookie sheets about 10 minutes in a 350°F oven.

CRISP SHRIMP WITH FRUIT SAUCE

A rather spectacular appetizer or first course that you can make entirely ahead. The sauce is equally delicious with cold meats.

**small shrimp (what you require
or can afford!)
1 cup all purpose flour
½ teaspoon baking powder**

**1 teaspoon salt
1 can beer (12 ounces)
solid shortening**

Shell shrimp, clean, but leave the tails on, and split longways, butterfly.

Mix together the flour, baking powder and salt, then slowly pour in the beer, whisking until smooth.

Put enough solid shortening in a heavy skillet to end up with 1½ inches, melted. Heat to 375°F or until a bread cube browns at once when put in.

Dip each shrimp in flour, shaking off excess, then in batter. Fry, a few at a time, in the hot fat to a golden color, not brown. Have ready a cake rack with brown paper on top. Drain the shrimp on this paper. Serve with fruit sauce.

 To reheat later: Put the shrimp on a paper topped cake rack in a 300°F oven until hot and crispy.

Fruit Sauce:

**1 cup orange marmalade
juice of ½ lemon
1 teaspoon Dijon mustard
1 teaspoon ground ginger
2 tablespoons horseradish**

Stir everything together. Set aside till serving time.

SAUSAGE CHEESE APPETIZERS

This makes a whole raft of appetizers with distinctive taste, and the great virtue of being freezable.

1 pound hot sausage   3 cups Bisquick
1 pound grated Cheddar cheese

Crumble the uncooked sausage, add the cheese and mix well. Blend in the Bisquick. Now shape into walnut size balls, and bake on ungreased cookie sheets for 10 minutes in a 350°F oven.

 If you freeze ahead, reheat at 350°F from a thawed state.

SCOTCH EGGS

Enormously popular all over Britain, these eggs can be bought in every shop that resembles a deli. In Harrod's great food halls in London, the Scotch egg department displays great trays of them. Cold, cut in half, they make excellent hors d' oeuvres.

6 eggs, hard boiled about 10   flour
   minutes   2 eggs, lightly beaten
1 pound well seasoned sausage   fine bread crumbs
   meat

Peel and lightly flour the eggs. Divide the sausage meat into 6 portions, then firmly shape the sausage around the eggs, covering them completely. Floured hands will help.

Flour again, lightly, dip in the beaten eggs and roll in the crumbs. Deep fry at 375°F until nicely browned. Drain on paper towels.

 No reason why you can't add favorite herbs to your sausage wrap. Chopped parsley, a bit of tarragon—you know.

BABY QUICHES

You wait and see—these get snapped up first at any party. Also, they freeze well and can be made in advance.

Shells:

½ cup butter or margarine   1 cup flour
1 package cream cheese (3 ounces)

Cream the butter and cream cheese together, then work in the flour. (If you normally use unsalted butter, put in a pinch of salt.) Chill the dough if too soft. Roll into 24 balls and press each one into a small muffin tin, making a shell.

Filling:

1 large egg, slightly beaten
½ cup milk
¼ teaspoon salt
1 cup grated Swiss cheese

Combine the egg, milk and salt. Divide the cheese among the little shells. Spoon the egg mixture in and bake at 350°F for 30 minutes.

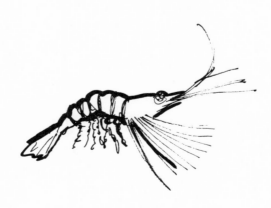

MINI QUICHE SHRIMP HORS d' OEUVRES

You'll get twenty four delicious appetizers from this recipe. It calls for the tiny muffin tins and shortcuts your work nicely by using packaged rolls.

12 refrigerator butterfly rolls, unbaked
1 cup small cooked shrimp or 1 can (4½ ounces)
1 egg, beaten
½ cup light cream
1 tablespoon brandy
½ teaspoon salt
dash pepper
1⅓ ounces Gruyère cheese

Grease 2 tiny muffin tins. Halve each dinner roll then press each half into the tins to form shells. Place several shrimp in each, dividing evenly.

Combine the beaten egg with the cream, brandy, salt and pepper. Divide among the shells using about 2 tablespoons in each. Slice the cheese into 24 little triangles, and put a piece on each shell.

Bake at 375°F for 20 minutes or until golden. You may serve at once, or cool, wrap in foil and freeze. To serve after freezing, reheat on a baking sheet for 10 minutes at 375°F.

WALNUT CHEESE MADEIRA MOLD

Aged in the mold, a smooth cum crunchy spread to make well ahead.

1 package cream cheese (8 ounces)
1 package Gruyère cheese (8 ounces)
3 tablespoons Madeira wine
½ cup coarsely chopped walnuts

Soften the cheeses, then combine them until well blended. Use the electric mixer for speed. Beat in the Madeira.

Find yourself a 2 cup plastic container, round, nice if it has sloping sides. Line the container with plastic wrap. Cover the bottom with half the walnuts. Spoon on half the cheese mixture, then the rest of the walnuts. Top with the rest of the cheese, pressing down to pack the mold smoothly. Cover with more plastic wrap and refrigerate 2 days.

To serve, unmold, unwrap and undeniably, enjoy.

 You may use dry sherry if you prefer.

Earning Your Stripes

Between the time you are a beginning cook and the day when you are an old pro, a number of things will happen to you in the kitchen that you won't read about in cook books.

In your arena, filled with flame and sharp knives and whirring blades, you will have some experiences that are off-putting to say the least. This is simply to reassure you that we have all had them.

At first you will burn yourself. Repeatedly. The first two weeks of my marriage I burned neat red stripes on both forearms putting things in the oven and taking them out. My first hash marks.

A little later, I cooked something in the oven in the beautiful smooth, old iron skillet my Mother had given me. I removed it from the oven to the burner, came back to finish the sauce, and took hold of the handle. Oh, my.

You will set fire to at least one potholder, perhaps only char it. And if you are inclined to wear flowing garments, you may indeed find yourself ablaze. One night I came into a friend's kitchen as she was reaching across her gas range, chatting to me animatedly, while the sleeve of her caftan burned merrily.

You will cut yourself with knives, the incredibly sharp edge of a ham can, a broken glass in the dishwater.

You will allow things to boil over. You may watch the pot for what seems an eternity waiting for it to boil, then you turn your back for a moment, and over it goes—spaghetti, shrimp, lima beans. The worst of these is shrimp. Nothing smells quite as revolting as that bubbling liquid when it hits the burner.

Correction: One thing is worse. The day will come when you put eggs on to hard cook, then answer the phone in another room. The aroma of cooked dry eggs lying brown in the pan is unforgettable.

You will, more than once, not turn the heat down under the spaghetti sauce soon enough, and from each of those round depressions that form on top will come a lively spurt of sauce. The range will be polka dotted with red.

You will klonk yourself on the head one day as you reach for something on the top shelf, and something else comes down with it.

You will rise two feet off the floor the day you absent mindedly stick a fork down the glowing toaster to retrieve the piece that didn't pop.

You will sadly watch cakes fall. You will make seven minute icing that isn't set in seven hours.

And then, there are the children, playing in the flour, rearranging all pots and pans. While we all know we must protect our children in the kitchen, that one works both ways.

I know a young woman who came into the kitchen one day and found her four year old just finishing an interesting piece of work. He had emptied every spice and herb jar into the sink, down the drain. He was, God help us, a climber.

As they get older they tend to take a finger full of cake icing as they pass by. They knock over something in the back of the refrigerator and the something goes drip, drip, then quietly hardens on the bottom. They take the best knife you have for crafts, for opening something or sawing through something else.

When my children were small, we still got milk in bottles. The house rule was that whoever finished the bottle, washed it. And while I don't want to mention names, somebody in our house would never quite finish the milk, but leave a token amount to avoid the chore. Right up the wall it drove me!

The day will come when you become deft and experienced. You won't cut or burn yourself, or boil things over, or shock yourself on the toaster. And by that time you will be cool in the kitchen, everything under control.

But never count on an incident-free life in your kitchen. Something waits to happen. It lurks there, knowing that one moment you won't be paying attention or that you did something too fast, and it will "getcha."

Like the day I watched my mother, who had been cooking for years and years, season an enormous pot of soup. She tilted the stove salt shaker over, gave a shake, and the whole top came off releasing about a half cup of salt. End of soup.

Go warily as you earn your stripes.

Soup de Jour...

Soups, Soupes, Zuppas *et al.*

There is an interesting little group of words we commonly use which are international—taxi, chocolate, coffee, the sort of thing where in most of the world some variant will get you what you're asking for.

Soup is such a word. It may be soupe, zuppa, soppa, or a number of other spellings, but the simple sound of it is universal. So is its appeal.

As the beginning of the meal or sometimes the meal itself, soup can be a true mainstay of your menu, for if bread is the staff of life, soup must certainly be its savor.

Never underestimate the power of the rich aromas of soup cooking. Second only to the smell of fresh bread baking, it establishes your house as home, alerts the appetites of your family and causes an upsurge in their esteem for you.

Case in point: my sister Irene, who is no slouch in any area, was canny enough, during the selling of a house, to arrange as many of the real estate showings as possible late in the afternoon. She would set the dining room table with all the elegance she could muster—then have something cooking that smelled wonderful.

Soup was the big favorite as a come-on. The house sold quickly, and I have always felt that soup had something to do with it.

Most soups start with stock, beef or chicken or fish. Beef stock may be light in color, achieved by cooking bones and some meat in water with a bouquet of vegetables. It may be brown stock, in which case you brown the bones first, then proceed. Chicken is easiest for us to stock up on since many dishes want poached or stewed chicken to start, salad for instance.

Not many people make fish stock, which is based on bones, heads and remains from the fish man. There is often a suggestion in a recipe to use clam juice instead, but I think it changes the taste too much. That famous Swiss company that makes the very good dehydrated soups puts out a fish stock that can be reconstituted in the same way, but I have never been able to get even my fancy grocer to stock it. If you see it, buy it.

It is well worth your time to make good stock since you can freeze it in pints or quarts and make soup at the drop of a noodle. Speaking of noodles, when you want to create a big, full meal soup, there are alternatives to pasta. You can use white beans or red beans, rice and potatoes. Sometimes when I make a cold soup and have no really heavy cream, I bake a potato, and toss in the meat of it, to thicken. In the case of strong flavored vegetables like broccoli, the potato will mellow it as well.

If you are freezing a big soup like a vegetable or a variant of minestrone, freeze it before you put in the pasta, and add the noodles or macaroni later. They change slightly under freezing, and since they cook so quickly, why not?

I am frequently chided for not telling readers how many people a pot of soup will serve. It all depends, I keep telling them. If that's the dinner, it's going to serve half as many as if it were the first course. If, on a summer night, you start with a small cup of icy soup, that changes the count again.

But here, may I suggest you make plenty of soup. We all know that many soups are better the second day, and if you're lucky enough to have some left over, freeze it.

It may be that you don't make lots of soup because you haven't got a big soup pot. That is something you really should have in your kitchen, not only for soup, but for cooking pasta, which wants gallons of water to cook properly.

Following are some soup recipes you may not have tried, all in family-size quantities. Try them on for taste.

CHILLED ASPARAGUS SOUP

This recipe allows you to have your cake and eat it too! Gloria Mark, who devised it, serves just the tips of asparagus in extravagant abandon when the good stuff is plentiful. Then she uses the middles of the stalks for this fine soup.

1 cup asparagus stalk middles
4 cooked tips
2 cups chicken broth

½ cup plain yogurt
¼ cup sour cream
chopped chives

Simmer asparagus middle pieces in the broth, covered, until really tender. Remove from heat and buzz about ½ cup at a time in the blender. Remove strings as you go. If the strings are all through the purée, force it through a sieve to catch them.

Chill the purée and, when ready to serve, swirl the yogurt through until well mixed. Taste for seasoning.

Serve in chilled bowls topped with a dollop of sour cream, an asparagus tip and a sprinkling of chives. Serves four.

CARROT SOUP

A great start for a winter meal. Or any meal.

3 cups grated carrots
¼ cup rice, slow cooking kind
1½ quarts good chicken stock
1 cup light cream

1 teaspoon salt
½ teaspoon cayenne pepper
2 tablespoons chopped parsley

Add carrots and rice to the chicken stock in a saucepan. Bring to a boil, then reduce to a simmer, cover and cook until the carrots are just tender and the rice is soft.

Purée in the blender or processor, then return to the saucepan. Add cream, salt and cayenne and blend well. Heat through and serve garnished with chopped parsley. Serves six.

GREEK LEMON SOUP

The first time I tasted this in Athens, it became one of my favorites—so light, so fresh on the tongue. It has the same ingredients as the famous lemon sauce you get over stuffed vine leaves, except for the rice and the proportions.

6 cups good chicken stock
4 tablespoons regular rice
4 large eggs separated, room temperature

salt to taste
4 tablespoons lemon juice
fresh ground pepper

Cook the rice in the chicken stock until it is tender, about 15 minutes. Take off the heat and remove one cup of the stock, setting the pot aside.

In the mixer bowl, beat the egg whites with the salt until they hold stiff peaks. Keep beating as you add the egg yolks then, very slowly, the lemon juice. Add the cup of stock in a slow stream, still beating.

Now pour the egg mixture into the soup pot and return to the lowest heat. Just heat through, stirring gently. If you heat too rapidly or bring to a boil, the mixture will separate. Season to taste. Serves six.

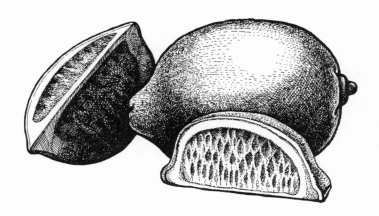

MINESTRONE

The vegetable soup of Italy comes in hundreds of ways and is a truly fertile area for you cooks who like to experiment.

When I was less experienced, I used to put everything but the kitchen sink in minestrone, along with meat. As I have learned more, the idea of a simpler soup has become more appealing, the taste of the fewer vegetables clearer, a refinement evident.

If you have good stock, you can start your minestrone with about a ¼ pound of salt pork diced, and cook the first seasonings in that—the onion and so on.

Many Italian soup makers start with a battuto, a finely chopped mixture of the salt pork, onion, celery, perhaps a carrot and whatever herb you choose—a sage leaf, some basil, whatever. It is tempting to think of doing this in the blender but it doesn't work very well. Chop by hand until you have almost a paste.

Then you put a little olive oil in the bottom of the kettle and sauté this paste to a golden color, stirring. Add your good stock and proceed from there, adding vegetables according to cooking time—or according to what you have on hand.

At the end when the soup has great savor, add the pasta or the white or red beans you fancy. The pasta needs to go in just for cooking time, and the canneloni, drained and rinsed, should go in only to be really heated through.

Recently, I have discovered how good red cabbage is in minestrone—you might try a cup of it chopped or sliced in the next soup pot.

Serve always with a bowl of grated Romano or Parmesan cheese to sprinkle over the top.

LOBSTER BISQUE, MARYLAND STYLE

The most absolutely elegant thing you can serve to start a lovely dinner party short of caviar. It should do for six rimmed soups, or eight cups.

2 cups boiled lobster meat
2 cups lobster stock

2 cups medium cream sauce
sherry wine to taste

Boil a 2 pound lobster in well salted water for 20 minutes. Remove the lobster, cool, then take the meat from the shell. Cut the meat in bite size pieces.

Boil the lobster shell for 30 minutes in 3 cups of water. Strain the stock—you should have 2 cups.

Make a medium cream sauce using:

2 cups evaporated milk
4 tablespoons flour
5 tablespoons butter

Combine lobster meat, stock and cream sauce and heat, stirring, adding sherry to taste.

 If you are serving in cups, cut the lobster meat rather small. There's nothing stranger than a great piece of something in a small cup.

ANNE'S CORN CHOWDER

Perfectly simple, perfectly delicious.

1 medium onion, chopped fine
1 stick butter or margarine
4 medium potatoes in half inch dice

3 cans cream style corn, medium size
1 pint half and half
1 pint milk

Sauté the onions, butter and potato together in a very deep skillet or a saucepan but do not brown. When the onions are limp, add just enough water to allow the potatoes to cook, then cover and cook until they are tender.

Add corn, cream and milk, stir together and season with salt and pepper. Bring almost to a boil and serve piping hot. Serves six to eight.

CREAMED MUSSEL SOUP

This is an exemplary soup, elegant, on only the finest menus, and yet it is very easy to make. It wants the freshest mussels. When served in grand restaurants the mussels are left out. At home I put them back in because they are good. On a menu, it may be called Billi-Bi.

2 pounds mussels
2 small onions, quartered
4 scallions, chopped
salt and fresh ground pepper
pinch of cayenne pepper
1 cup dry white wine

3 tablespoons butter
½ bay leaf
¼ teaspoon thyme
2 cups heavy cream
1 egg yolk, beaten

Scrub the mussels vigorously to remove beards, sand and silt. Place in a large kettle with the onions, scallions, salt and peppers, wine, butter, bay leaf and thyme.

Cover and bring to a boil, then reduce the heat and steam 5 to 10 minutes, checking to see when the mussels have all opened. If any are unopened after 10 minutes, discard them.

Remove the mussels and set aside. Strain the broth through a cheesecloth lined sieve.

Put the strained broth back in the saucepan, making certain there are no miniscule bits of shell lurking there. Bring the liquid just to the boil, then add the cream. Bring back to a boil and remove at once from the heat. Add the mussels. Pour a little hot liquid into the beaten egg yolk, stir, then return it to the pot. It will thicken slightly almost at once. If you put it back on the heat, do not let it boil.

Serve hot or ice cold.

CANADIAN PEA SOUP

Called Habitant in Canada, this heavy, nourishing soup is a first cousin to Swedish Pea Soup. You need large dried yellow peas, and of course, it's good if you have lean pork.

1 pound dried whole yellow peas
2½ quarts of water
½ pound salt pork, rind off, rinsed and dried

2 medium onions, coarsely chopped
1 carrot, diced
1 teaspoon salt
½ teaspoon dried sage

Rinse the peas, discarding the dark ones or any little stones. Put them in a heavy soup kettle and add the water. Bring to a boil for 2 minutes, then remove from the heat and allow to stand in the hot water for 1 hour.

Cut the salt pork into tiny dice, and render in a skillet for about 10 minutes or until golden brown and crisped. Remove from the skillet with a slotted spoon and put on paper towels to remove the fat.

Put the peas in the water back on the heat, bring to a boil and if necessary, skim the top. Add the pork and all the other ingredients and simmer for about 2 hours, stirring occasionally. The soup should be thick. Taste for seasoning and serve. Serves eight.

BAKED POTATO SOUP

Some winter night, delight your loved ones with a big tureen of this rich soup—you won't need much else!

4 large Idaho potatoes
4 cans cream of chicken soup
¾ cup water
1 cup light cream
1 cup heavy cream

salt, fresh ground pepper to taste
2 tablespoons butter (or more if you like)
chopped chives

Bake the potatoes, being sure they are well done and mealy. Cut in half and remove from skins, then mash up in an enamel saucepan.

Heat the chicken soup diluted with the water, then add it to the potatoes gradually, stirring to make a smooth mixture. Add the creams, salt and pepper to taste and bring back just to the boil. Stir in the butter and sprinkle with chives to serve. Serves six.

 If you want a really smooth soup, mash the potatoes with the mixer, not the food processor which makes the potatoes rather gluey.

ROCK FISH CHOWDER

A treasured recipe given to me by Tunie Wright who cooks up a storm each year for the Charlestown, Maryland, Colonial Fair. I think it's the best fish chowder I have ever eaten.

3 to 4 pounds rock fish, dressed
4 to 6 potatoes, peeled and diced
1 large onion, chopped
2 or 3 stalks celery, chopped
1 small carrot, diced
crushed red pepper
salt and black pepper

chopped parsley
evaporated milk
a big chunk of butter
3 hard cooked eggs, chopped
sherry to taste
1 small can cream style corn, optional

Boil the fish until it is flaky tender. Remove skin and dark meat which is too oily and strong. Separate the fish into chunks and set aside.

In a large saucepan, cook the diced vegetables in water to cover until tender. Add the fish, red pepper, salt and pepper, parsley and enough evaporated milk to make the consistency you like. Add the butter and chopped eggs, and if you choose, the creamed corn. Reheat but do not boil. Add sherry to taste, and serve. Serves eight.

BLAZE'S PUMPKIN SOUP

Rich but inexpensive soup to warm up a winter night. Canned pumpkin? Of course you can use it.

2 tablespoons chopped shallots
2 tablespoons butter
2 cups chicken stock
2 cups mashed, cooked pumpkin
2 tablespoons flour kneaded
    with 2 tablespoons butter

½ cup light cream
1 teaspoon ground mace
salt, white pepper
garlic croutons
chopped chives

Sauté the shallots in butter until soft but not brown, stirring often. Now, combine them with the stock, pumpkin, cream, mace, salt and pepper in a large saucepan. Put over heat and, and as the soup comes to a boil, pinch off bits of the flour-butter thickening and add to the pot. Simmer until they cook and give the soup body. Serve garnished with croutons and chives.

Sometimes you do not achieve the thickness you want in a soup or stew. The addition of little balls of flour and butter is a flavorful, sure way to get it, lump free.

WALTER'S POTATO SOUP

Hot in the winter, chilled in the summer, a versatile soup, inexpensive to make and very good going down.

3 tablespoons butter
2 large onions, sliced
2 pounds potatoes, peeled and
    sliced
3 cups milk

3 cups chicken stock
1 cup light cream
salt and fresh ground pepper
chopped chives

Melt the butter in a large saucepan, add the sliced onions and cook over low heat until golden. Add potatoes, stock and milk, then season with salt and pepper. Cook until tender.

Put the mixture through the blender or your food processor until smoothly pureed. Return to the saucepan and add the cream. Reheat without boiling. Top with chives and serve. Or, chill, top with chives and serve.

 I would say this would serve six, hot, on a winter's night, eight, chilled in a cup, on a summer's night.

VIRGINIA'S TOMATO-ORANGE SOUP

Served hot or cold it is the most beautifully colored soup you can imagine!

1 small onion, chopped
2 tablespoons butter
2 tablespoons flour
2 cans Italian tomatoes, drained, chopped (35 ounces)

5 cups chicken broth
3 juice oranges, sliced, peel left on, seeded
2 cups dry white wine
2 cups heavy cream

In a heavy saucepan, sauté the onions in the butter until tender then sprinkle with the flour to make a roux. Cook briefly, then add the tomatoes and chicken broth. Bring to a boil, then simmer down to ½ the original quantity, uncovered, of course. This will take about 1 hour. (So, make the dessert!)

Strain the tomato broth and return the liquid to the soup pan. In the food processor, process the oranges and wine, then strain this through a fine sieve into the broth. If you use a blender, chop the oranges up first.

Add the heavy cream and season to taste with salt and pepper. Chill and serve as is, or serve hot with a dollop of sour cream garnished with a bit of grated orange rind. Serves eight.

COLD SPINACH SOUP

A dandy first course . . . and very pretty.

1 pound fresh spinach
2 scallions, minced, include some green
2½ cups chicken broth

salt and pepper
few gratings of nutmeg
1 cup sour cream

Wash the spinach well and remove the stems. Cut up the leaves coarsely and cook them with the scallions in the broth for about 5 minutes. Purée in the blender. Season to taste with salt and pepper and nutmeg. Stir in the sour cream and chill. Served in ice cold bowls to six.

CURRIED PEA SOUP, COLD

This soup is so much liked by friends that they suggest it be on the menu, plaintively request it when they're ill, and lap it up when they're well.

1½ cups fresh shelled peas or 1 package frozen peas
1 medium potato, peeled, cut up
1 medium onion, coarsely chopped

2 cups good chicken stock
1 cup light cream
salt and curry powder to taste

Put peas, potatoes, onion and 1 cup of the stock in a saucepan. Cook until tender, then purée in the blender or processor.

Add remaining stock and cream and combine well. Season with salt, then add the curry powder, starting with one teaspoon and adding more to your liking. Chill. Serves six.

Everything In Its Season

They say that when a student is beginning to learn to play the organ, he is so dazzled by all the tonal possibilities of the myriad of stops, that he keeps adding effect on effect, ending up with no effect.

The beginning herb and spice user can run amok the same way, tossing in dashes with abandon. Creating.

On the other hand, my sister crossed the Atlantic in a Polish ship shortly after World War II, a ship that was pretty well geared to ethnic travelers. She has never eaten a caraway seed since.

Somewhere in between, there is a delicate use of herbs and spices that neither astounds nor cloys.

Of all the herbs, basil, dill and parsley are my favorites. Parsley grows everywhere in abundance and is always available. It adds flavor to many dishes, and as a garnish appears in maybe a quarter of the recipes you read. It keeps well in a tightly covered jar, or you can snip it up or chop in the food processor and freeze.

Dill, a feathery, delicate herb doesn't hold up as well but gives a very distinctive flavor to whatever. If you have it more than a few days, snip up and freeze. When you use dill in cooking, unlike other herbs, it loses flavor. Reserve some of the amount and put in just at the end. I love it sprinkled on new potatoes, buttered carrots, and especially it belongs with fish.

Basil is so redolent that if you have it in the garden, you get a great whiff of it when it rains. It appears in many Italian dishes, tastes wonderful on fresh tomatoes, and is the basis for pesto, a pasta sauce *extraordinaire*. You can preserve fresh basil in olive oil: wash and dry the leaves, then layer in a jar with just a bit of salt on each layer. Pack firmly then cover with good olive oil. They will darken but not lose flavor. (Do peeled garlic cloves the same way. You'll never throw out another withered little pod.)

There are countless herbs and spices and when you start to use them don't go blindly. Taste. Before you put a big teaspoon in, put a pinch on a tablespoon of whatever you're cooking. Some spices give such a jolt to a dish that if it's new to you, you should experiment before you find it isn't to your liking. One of the most distinctive spices is curry powder which is not a spice but a combination of a about fifteen spices. Curry is something you like or can't abide—nothing in between. Have a care.

Herbs and spices in jars don't get better, they just get older. Check through now and again, because that green bay leaf isn't going to do much for you if it has turned beige. When the dried marjoram is coffee colored, replace it.

A standard kitchen phenomenon happens in the spice cabinet. Have you ever seen a woman going unerringly to an herb or spice jar without groping or knocking over three or four other jars in the process? In otherwise meticulously ordered kitchens, the spice cabinets often make no rhyme or reason.

Some rainy day, sort them out. Put the ones you use frequently in one place, the others somewhere else. Of course, when you put them back—think.

Some day I'm going to have a narrow little shelf put the whole way round my kitchen, resting on the splash board. Then I'll have a single row in alphabetical order.

Some day.

The Tearing of the Green...

Salads

Although it may come up only rarely in your life, a discussion about salads almost always devolves upon whether it should be Before, During or After.

The first time I ever had salad before an entree was in California, and that was years ago. Even then I had the somewhat cheated feeling that all that green had taken away some of my interest in the principal dish that followed.

Today, restaurants serve salad first to keep you from complaining while you wait for the cooked part. I don't eat it unless I am ravenous.

On the other hand, you have the Francophile who regards you as illiterate and insensible if you serve the salad along with the entree. It must come after. It cleanses the palate, gets you ready for cheese and cake, and all that jazz.

Well, sometimes I want my salad with my dinner. Sometimes I want it after—but never before.

The French salad is almost always a small plate of greens with a simple French dressing. In St. Emilion once, I had the best dressing ever, and it was made at tableside by the attentive, gentle waiter. He had a saucer, poured in some oil and vinegar, inquired, "Mustard?", added it. Then with a few deft strokes he put it together, with a fork yet. It was perfect.

It probably only took him about 20 years to get that act together.

Salad rules are simple once you decide whether you belong to the Before, During or After School. Greens should be young, tender and crisp. Vegetables garnishes should be crisp and colorful—the beauty of a salad adds immeasurably to the diner's enjoyment.

The dressing should lightly coat, not drown. Garlic should be removed. Onions should be sliced paper thin, not chopped. Croutons should be crisp and fresh, and not store-bought.

The worst salad days of my life were on a small Greek ship where there was great confusion in the cuisine. While we occasionally had a fine dish, the menu was tourist, and a mess. While the Greek crew was probably eating green salad with Feta cheese—superb—we received every evening a bowl containing chopped cabbage and carrots. That was it. It's a wonder we didn't get scurvy.

When we got to Istanbul, we said, "God bless Conrad", hared it to the Hilton, and had the biggest bowl of greens and fresh shrimp I ever saw.

But there are many salads that are not just greens. Fruit salads, composed salads, salad plates that make a meal. Coleslaw is a salad for fish—and often for Thanksgiving turkey.

You may eat cottage cheese if you like but it's not my cup of tea. It doesn't taste bad, just blah. But if you want a brilliant idea, pick up on this one which I enjoyed at the famous Greenbrier Hotel.

After a superb entree, they brought an attractive green salad on a rather large plate, and alongside, we had cheese. They passed more good French bread, filled the glasses, and everyone enjoyed a lovely, leisurely course. I think that's a great idea.

But whether you use crisp iceberg, sturdy romaine, delicate watercress, zingy escarole—whatever greens—do try to get yourself a salad spinner to dry the greens perfectly. It makes a great difference in your salads and is relatively inexpensive.

BEAN AND BACON SALAD

This recipe came from a local cookbook put out by the Milford, Delaware, women's hospital auxiliary, a book which raised a great deal of money for the local hospital.

1 pound fresh green beans
½ cup onions, chopped
⅓ cup salad oil
¼ cup vinegar
½ teaspoon salt, fresh ground pepper
4 hard cooked eggs, chopped
¼ cup mayonnaise

1 teaspoon prepared mustard
2 teaspoons vinegar
dash of salt
4 slices bacon, fried crisp, crumbled
greens
paprika

Cook the beans until tender crisp in salted water. Drain and while still warm, combine with onions, salad oil, vinegar, salt and pepper. Toss lightly, cover and chill.

In a small bowl, combine eggs, mayonnaise, mustard, vinegar and salt. Cover and chill.

Just before serving, toss the beans with the bacon crisps and arrange nicely on salad greens. Top with a spoonful of the egg mixture and color with paprika. Serves six.

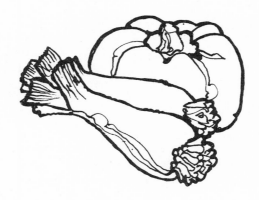

ORANGE GELATIN MOLD

In the Thirties, when I was, oh, so young, there was a big food fad for gelatin salads, and most of us who lived through it were constantly overexposed to items like Sunshine Salad, grated carrot and crushed pineapple in orange or lemon gelatin. Then, in the Forties when the mass of Americans discovered the simple green salad, we revolted against canned fruit suspended in fruit gel with miniature marshmallows.

But somewhere in between, there is still room for very pleasant molds where the base is fruit gelatin. This is a particularly pretty and pleasing one.

1 package orange gelatin
1 cup boiling water
¼ cup fresh orange juice

1 package cream cheese (8 ounce size)

Dissolve the gelatin in the boiling water and add the orange juice. Put in the blender or processor with the cream cheese and buzz until smooth. Chill in a small mold until set. (Double the recipe for a ring mold.)

Serve with fresh fruit.

SOUR CREAM COLESLAW

1 pint sour cream
2 egg yolks
¼ cup lemon juice
¼ cup horseradish
½ teaspoon paprika
2 to 3 teaspoons French's mustard

1 teaspoon sugar
2 teaspoons salt
2 quarts finely shredded cabbage

Combine the sour cream with well beaten egg yolks. Blend in the remaining ingredients and simply pour over the cabbage, tossing to coat all over. Refrigerate at least 1 hour. Serves six to eight.

WATERCRESS SALAD PRAGOFF

Hot salad dressing? Just try it. You'll like it.

3   bunches fresh watercress, washed, trimmed, dried, chilled.

The dressing:

6 slices bacon
2 eggs
1 teaspoon Dijon mustard
3 tablespoons lemon juice

2 tablespoons white vinegar
2 tablespoons sugar
salt and fresh ground pepper

Sauté bacon slices until crisp, then drain, cool and crumble. Set aside.

In a heavy enamel pan, whisk together eggs, mustard, lemon juice, vinegar and sugar, making sure everything is well blended. Do not cook. Season to taste.

When you are ready to serve, place the watercress in a salad bowl with the bacon bits. Put the saucepan over high heat and cook the dressing, stirring vigorously until it is thick and smooth. Caution: You must not let it boil.

As soon as the dressing is thick, plunge the pan into cold water to stop the cooking. Spoon the hot dressing over the cress and gently fold it in. Serve immediately.

MY OWN GREEN BEAN ROMAINE SALAD

Romaine and bibb lettuce are my favorite greens. With an elaborate dinner, bibb with just a touch of fine French dressing is the perfect salad. Romaine, on the other hand is sturdy enough to take all sorts of good additions. Like this one.

Cook some green beans the usual way, drain and marinate in French or Italian dressing.

Hard cook some eggs, one to a customer, chill and peel when ready to assemble the salad.

Cut the romaine—or tear if you want—into bite size pieces and arrange on salad plates. Top with green beans on one side, egg wedges on the other, and over all the creamy Italian dressing.

Creamy Italian Dressing

¾ cup mayonnaise
1 tablespoon wine vinegar
1 tablespoon lemon juice
1 tablespoon salad oil
1 tablespoon water
1 teaspoon Worcestershire
    sauce
½ teaspoon oregano
1 teaspoon sugar
1 small garlic clove, minced

Just mix it all together very well, and chill.

NIECE JANE'S SALAD

A big salad for a party or picnic that you can really make a day ahead. Cut back for family use.

1 head lettuce, washed, dried, torn	1 pound bacon, fried crisp, crumbled
1 pound fresh spinach, stemmed	6 hard cooked eggs, diced
1 bunch green onions, chopped	1 box frozen peas, not cooked

Make sure all the greens are dry, then put in a giant bowl and toss all ingredients.

Dressing:

1 small package Hidden Valley Ranch mix	1 cup mayonnaise
	1 cup sour cream

Mix together and spread over the top of the greens as if you were icing a cake. Be certain everything is covered, then stretch plastic wrap tightly over the bowl. The salad will be crisp and delicious twenty four hours later. Toss to serve.

CELERY CABBAGE SLAW

An alternative to coleslaw you might find pleasing. From Bea Hrab.

3 cups shredded celery cabbage

Dressing:

¼ cup white vinegar	fresh ground pepper to your taste
3 tablespoons vegetable oil	
2 tablespoons sugar	½ teaspoon dry mustard
1 teaspoon salt	1 teaspoon grated onion

Blend all dressing ingredients well and pour over the chopped or shredded cabbage. Chill well before serving. Serves four to six.

CONTINENTAL POTATO SALAD

When I was living in London I frequented a wine bar, that stellar institution where you can get a fine lunch at the bar and good wine by the glass. The owner made potato salad the British way for which he didn't peel the little new potatoes but used them cooked with their pink jackets on. He also made this fresh, French tasting salad.

6 medium sized new potatoes	4 tablespoons olive oil
1 teaspoon salt	¼ teaspoon dry mustard
few grinds of pepper	1 tablespoon chopped parsley
1½ tablespoons white wine vinegar	1 teaspoon dried tarregon (or dill or basil)

Boil the potatoes with their skins on until tender. Put under cold water, drain and peel. Slice thinly in a serving bowl.

Combine salt, pepper, vinegar and oil and beat in the mustard to make a dressing. Toss with the potatoes until they are well covered. Let come to room temperature, then add the chopped herbs, toss, and serve. This is not served cold, but at room temperature. Will do for four to six.

QUICKIE TOMATO ASPIC

This is so ridiculously simple, it's almost embarrassing to set down.

Bring 2 cups of tomato juice, plain or seasoned, to a boil and use it instead of water in 1 package of lemon gelatin. Stir to dissolve, pour into a square cake pan or small loaf pan and chill.

 If you like, add sliced, olives, chopped celery and/or green pepper when the aspic has set slightly. If you're dieting, it works with the diet gelatin as well.

THREE VEGETABLE SALAD

Here's an engaging switch from the ubiquitous three bean salad one encounters rather too many places! Make a day ahead.

1 can green peas, drained (16 ounce size)
1 can whole kernel corn, drained (12 ounce size)
1 can French cut green beans, drained (16 ounce size)

1 medium onion, chopped
½ cup chopped celery
¼ cup diced pimento

Marinade:

½ cup vegetable oil
½ cup white wine vinegar
¾ cup sugar

1 teaspoon salt
fresh ground pepper to your liking

Combine all marinade ingredients in a saucepan and heat just to boiling. Cool.

Lightly mix all salad ingredients in a largish bowl then dress with the marinade. In twenty four hours, you'll have a fine and pretty sweet-and-sour salad.

It keeps well so don't worry about the quantity.

SAUERKRAUT SALAD

From The Corner Cupboard, an inn in Rehoboth, Delaware, one of their fine homemade style goodies. This makes a good relish or salad and will keep well for a long time. Wonderful on a hot dog sandwich.

1 large can or bag of sauerkraut, well drained
1 small onion, finely chopped
1 large green pepper, finely chopped
¾ cup celery, chopped
1 small jar pimentos, drained, cut up
½ cup salad oil
½ cup vinegar
¼ cup water
1¼ cups sugar

Blend everything together. Let stand for at least twenty four hours and serve, chilled.

If you find the rather acrid taste of sauerkraut brine trying, you might even rinse it off, then drain well and proceed.

CUCUMBER MOUSSE

Pretty as a picture, this mold for a buffet or a summer luncheon.

1 package lime gelatin (3 ounces)
¾ cup boiling water
1 envelope unflavored gelatin
¼ cup cold water
1 cup mayonnaise
1 tablespoon minced onion
1 cup cottage cheese
1 medium cucumber, peeled, chopped
3 dashes of Tabasco sauce
1 garlic clove, minced
½ cup slivered almonds
optional: green food coloring

Dissolve lime gelatin in the boiling water, then the plain gelatin in the cold water. (Separately.)

In the processor or blender, put the mayonnaise, onion, cottage cheese, cucumber, Tabasco, garlic and almonds. Blend or process well, then add both gelatins. Blend or process again.

If you like, add a few drops of green food coloring to enhance the appearance, then turn into your favorite mold lightly greased with mayonnaise. Chill overnight. Serve on greens to six.

POPPY SEED DRESSING

I had this salad dressing on a fruit plate in a Florida restaurant. They were kind enough to add to the collection!

1½ cups sugar
2 teaspoons dry mustard
1½ teaspoons salt
⅔ cup white vinegar

3 tablespoons onion juice
2 cups corn oil
3 tablespoons poppy seeds

Combine sugar, salt, mustard and vinegar in the small mixer bowl. Add onion juice and stir to combine. Now, on low speed, mix as you slowly add the oil in a gentle stream. The mixture will thicken, but after it does, continue to beat for at least 5 minutes more. Add the poppy seeds and beat for another minute. Store, covered, in the refrigerator.

 Onion juice? Put an onion in the blender or processor, reduce to practically pulp, then strain, averting your eyes. If the dressing should separate, pour off the clear part and beat again, adding the thick mixture slowly to the thin.

FRENCH DRESSING

2 garlic cloves, halved	1 tablespoon cold water
1 teaspoon salt	scant ½ cup wine vinegar
½ teaspoon fresh ground pepper	olive oil
1 tablespoon sugar	
1 tablespoon Dijon type prepared mustard	

You must use a pint jar with a lid for this.

Put into the jar the garlic, salt, pepper, sugar and mustard. Add the tablespoon of cold water and just under a half cup wine vinegar. Then—shake like mad.

Now pour enough olive oil into the jar so that it comes up to an inch below the top. Again shake well, and let sit twenty four hours before using.

Give a shake before using each time. Do not store this in the refrigerator. It keeps just fine on the shelf.

BIG SUR SALAD DRESSING

To make an extraordinary salad out of just fresh greens, assemble this California style dressing which will do for several large bowls.

In the blender or food processor, blend until smooth:

6 anchovies	grated rind of 1 lemon
3 chopped scallions or shallots	1 teaspoon Worcestershire sauce
⅔ cup chopped cooked shrimp	
⅓ cup lemon juice	

Add to this mixture:

2⅔ cups mayonnaise

Combine well and serve over greens.

AUNT ELLEN'S SALAD DRESSING

1 teaspoon flour
1 teaspoon salt
½ cup sugar
¼ teaspoon dry mustard
3 tablespoons vinegar

½ cup water
1 egg
dash pepper
piece of butter

Sift flour, salt, sugar and dry mustard together in a saucepan. Add vinegar, water and egg to the saucepan and mix well.

Add a dash of pepper.

Cook over low heat until the sauce thickens, stirring all the time. Remove from the heat and cool to just warm, then add a dollop of butter. Refrigerate until used.

 We used to call this boiled dressing. It makes very good coleslaw.

MISSISSIPPI QUEEN SALAD DRESSING

Karla Tober took a trip on the famous riverboat, fell for the salad dressing and wheedled it out of the chef. It's delightful, a big recipe, but you'll eat it up quickly.

1 quart Hellman's mayonnaise
   (no substitute)
⅓ cup cold water
2 tablespoons dill weed
2 tablespoons black pepper
2 tablespoons grated Parmesan
   cheese
1 garlic clove, finely minced

1 teaspoon monosodium
   glutamate
3 tablespoons lemon juice
1 small onion, finely minced
2 tablespoons cider vinegar
Worcestershire and Tabasco to
   taste—a few drops?
salt to taste

Put it all together, it spells delicious. It should sit at least an hour, longer if possible. Store in the refrigerator. Lash over any green salad.

LUDDY'S PARSLEY DRESSING

To enhance good thick slices of summer's best tomatoes, try this tangy dressing. It keeps well, covered, in the refrigerator.

Into your blender or processor put:

2 cups parsley sprigs
½ cup chopped chives
1 cup sweet pickles, drained

2 garlic cloves
salt and fresh ground pepper

Blend or process, then add:

½ cup olive oil
½ cup red wine vinegar

¼ cup tarragon vinegar
sugar to taste

Mix well and allow to stand at room temperature, covered, for twenty four hours. After that, refrigerate. Makes 2 cups.

FRUITY FRENCH DRESSING

Every time this is served, someone wants the recipe. A fresh, lively tang over greens, and especially fine with orange and onion salad. This keeps well so don't worry about the quantity.

In the electric mixer, beat together:

2 cups salad oil
½ cup vinegar

In a small bowl, mix together:

½ teaspoon salt
½ cup confectioners sugar

1 teaspoon dry mustard
1 teaspoon paprika

Beat into the oil and vinegar, then add, stirring in:

1 teaspoon Worcestershire
    sauce
1 garlic clove, cut in half

juice of 2 oranges
juice of 1 lemon

Store in a large jar with a lid in the refrigerator.

Happenings

Suddenly—Himself comes home from work, checks out the kitchen, says, "What's that?", lifts a lid from a pan and announces, "I had that for lunch."

Suddenly—small Susie with one tooth out begins to cry at the breakfast table because she forgot to tell you this is the PTA bake sale day, and she needs a cake by 11:00 A.M. or she is ruined scholastically and socially.

Suddenly—the phone rings at 4:30 P.M. and it is husband cheerfully announcing that he's bringing home for dinner his man from Brussels, and should he pick up some wine, all the while you are trying to think of a wine that would go well with the hamburgers that are defrosting.

The great cooks work in shelter. They create in spotless, stainless steel kitchens and testing laboratories, architect designed oases where the serenity is broken only by an occasional pop or fizz or the discreet whirring of class equipment. The great have time to do picky-picky shopping, and also have one or more gnomes to clean up after.

(This does not include working chefs who live from crisis to crisis much as you do.)

You work in the busiest place in the house with a very high traffic count, a high decibel count as cabinets are slammed, and pots and pans dragged out by the floor baby, and very high emergency risk when your best laid plans are shot full of holes—as above.

Unless you wish to age prematurely, you have to keep one jump ahead. Your grandmother did this with her pantry full of things she had put up. Your mother kept ahead of the game with shelves of canned and boxed foods. But you have the best of all worlds—the shelves and the freezer.

We tend to think of the freezer as the boon of the large family, but from my own experience, it is equally valuable to the couple or loner. They always have more left over to freeze and since many are fully employed, have less time to cook.

One of the most important aspects of home freezing is marking the date clearly on the package or container. If you have a self defrosting box it is especially vital. I have noted that foods dry out and lose flavor more quickly in my new frost-free than they did in the old box I had to defrost manually.

You know best what to keep in your freezer. But to supplement it, you still need that pantry shelf for the tomatoes, mushrooms, cream soups, pimentos, olives, tuna, store bought marinara sauce, and a handful of cocktail snacks.

In the refrigerator, never run out of cheese, garlic, butter or margarine, milk or eggs. Like a good merchant, keep a running inventory.

Traumas will still arise. On a Friday afternoon, a distant cousin from out of town will call and say, "We're just here for the night but we'd love to see you." This, if you know your cousin means, "We're coming for dinner."

Close friends come for a drink. It's fun and nobody shows any sign of leaving. Your affable spouse suddenly, horrifyingly says, "Why don't you stay for supper—we're having such a good time."

This one actually happened to me. One Saturday afternoon when my daughter was about five, little girls with nicely wrapped gifts began to arrive at the house. Nancy had invited them to a birthday party. It wasn't even her birthday! So you have a party. Somehow. And send back the presents.

You are not cooking in a delightful vacuum but in a vital world where anything can happen and frequently does.

Fish Story

Check his eyes. Are they bright, clear and bulgy? Is his flesh firm and elastic and does he have a fine, fresh smell? If he does, and his scales are tight to the body, buy him.

You've got yourself a good fresh fish.

Once you've got your fish, cook him right away, the sooner the better. Fish will keep in the refrigerator in a cooked condition much longer than raw. So if you have a fisherman in your family, be ready to cook or freeze. Fish require a zero degree temperature to maintain flavor and moisture, and they should not be kept in the freezer more than six months.

Most of us, regrettably, get fish from the store, in which case the best thing to cultivate is a deep warm friendship with the fish man.

Generally, one should keep an open mind about what kind of fish so that one can get the best of the day. Your choice, of course, devolves on how you plan to cook.

Large fish: The commonest method is to bake, stuffed or unstuffed. As a rule of thumb, 10 minutes a pound in a 400°F oven is about right. The infallible test for doneness is if the fish flakes.

Poaching: A center cut of salmon or other large fish may be poached in salt water with lemon, or with any number of herbs and spices added. Wrapping in cheesecloth holds it together, and it should sit on a rack. Time depends on the bulk of the fish.

Broiling: If you broil whole flat fish, they need about 10 minutes a side and want some butter spread over. Fillets placed three to five inches away from the broiler unit simply need to brown one side, then the other. Some people put a slice of bacon over, but I prefer the less positive flavor of butter or even oil.

Charcoal Grilling: You need a hinged double grill to do thin fish over the coals—they're too hard to turn otherwise. Over the coals, fish want a marinade or they will dry out. About five inches above the coals is safe, 10 to 18 minutes according to thickness.

Frying: For deep frying, fish is coated with crumbs or batter as it is for pan frying. Do only one layer at a time in the skillet. This is the fastest and most popular way to do fillets, taking about 8 or 9 minutes for both sides.

Oven Browning: Just as you do chicken, you can do fish fillets, dipped in milk, then crumbs, and baked in a hot oven for 10 to 15 minutes. Temperature, 475°F.

Low in calories, delicate in flavor, fish can give your menu great variety. Cold, it makes delicious salads. Hot, as an entree, it generally looks more appealing with a colorful garnish, tastes better with a sauce, whether it's the routine tartar or some subtle concoction.

Lemon, and even orange juice, serve as delicate marinades for fish, and a wedge of lemon is almost de rigueur with all the finny creatures.

Some people have strange prejudices against some poor fish, the cat fish for instance, when actually it is sweet and white and very tender. Expand your fish menu. There's more in life than a flounder.

To me, the aristocracy of the sea is shellfish, and I am hard put to name the best.

The best crab I ever ate was simply beautiful lump, heated in butter in a skillet, served on toast. Shrimp is superior, cooked with a little bite left in and consumed cold, without guilt, since it is so low-cal. Mussels. The best were in Belgium where they were served right in the enameled cooking pot, steamed over a bed of vegetables, and eaten with French fries dipped in mustard and a cold, cold beer.

Oysters. From the day I was forced, literally, to eat a raw one, I have been an unflagging fan. A big plate of blue points can send me into rapture. And when the big babies are pan fried and served in our unique, regional way with a fresh made chicken salad, I enjoy, truly.

When you can afford the tiny bay scallops, they are tender and delicate to serve, just ever so lightly broiled in butter.

Ahead you will find a number of ways to prepare fish and shellfish. Enjoy.

Fish

THE COD FISH DISH
BELGIAN WATERZOOI

We're most accustomed to the chicken waterzooi, a sort of lemony stew that is eaten as a main course. But this one comes right from Amelie Fontaine who lives in Belgium and makes this frequently. They use fish called lott, but she thinks cod will do well.

3 small onions, chopped
1 garlic clove, minced
3 carrots, chopped

1 celery stalk, chopped
pinch of thyme

Melt a few tablespoons of butter in the bottom of a heavy, rather large pot, and sauté the chopped vegetables for about 20 minutes. Season with thyme.

1 cup dry white wine plus ¼ cup
**   water**
2 to 3 pounds cod

juice of a large lemon
3 leeks, washed well, chopped
salt and pepper to taste

Cut the cod into serving size pieces. Add the wine, lemon juice and leeks to the pot, then put in the fish. Simmer for 20 minutes, then thicken slightly with cornstarch.

While it cooks, beat together:

1 cup cream
2 egg yolks

Take the stew from the heat, and finish by adding the cream and egg mixture. If you must reheat, do not boil.

Serve in rimmed soup plates or bowls garnished with chopped celery.

When the waterzooi is served, a bowl of hot small potatoes is passed, and each person adds some to his bowl.

If you use two pounds of cod, it should serve four or five; three pounds should serve six to eight.

CRUSTY BAKED FISH

Tender fish fillets with a zesty crumb topping.

2 pounds fish fillets, 2 inches
   thick
salt and pepper
2 cups soft bread crumbs

6 tablespoons melted butter
2 tablespoons minced scallions
2 tablespoons lemon juice
2 teaspoons Dijon mustard

Make the fillets into four servings, however you can.

In a saucepan, melt the butter then add the scallions, lemon juice and mustard. Mix together, then toss the crumbs in the butter.

Season the fillets with salt and pepper lightly, then press the crumb mixture firmly on the top. Bake at 350°F for 15 to 20 minutes until you can flake the fish with a fork. Run the fish under the broiler to brown the crust lightly.

ROLLED FILLET OF FLOUNDER

Very dressed up fish with a delicate, rich flavor.

6 fillets of flounder
salt and pepper
1 medium onion, chopped
½ pound mushrooms, chopped
butter

2 cans tiny shrimp, drained
1 cup light cream
2 tablespoons flour
½ cup dry white wine
½ cup shredded Swiss cheese

Salt and pepper the fish. Sauté the onions and mushrooms in butter until tender, then stir in the shrimp and heat through.

Spoon filling over the large end of the fillets, dividing evenly and saving out some for the sauce. Roll up the fillets and arrange, seam side down, in a baking dish.

Stir the flour into the remaining stuffing, then add the cream and wine. Taste for seasoning, then heat just to the boiling point and pour over the fish. Sprinkle with cheese. Bake at 400°F 20 to 25 minutes until lightly browned and puffed. Serves three if the fillets are small, more if they are large.

BAKED HALIBUT MARCEL

Sister Irene had this at a Florida country club and was able to latch on to the recipe. It's good.

2 tablespoons butter
10 medium mushrooms, sliced
2 tablespoons paprika
1 pint fish stock
6 ounces dry sherry

2 pounds halibut steaks
salt and pepper
butter
2 cups medium cream sauce
grated Parmesan cheese

Sauté mushrooms in butter. In a minute or two, add paprika and the fish stock and simmer over low heat about 10 minutes. Add sherry.

Bake the halibut in a 350°F oven, seasoned and laced with some melted butter. Cover with foil. You don't want it brown. Bake until it flakes with a fork. The time will vary with the thickness of the steaks.

Remove fish from the oven and cool, then flake into a well-buttered casserole along with the mushroom mixture. Combine, then pour the cream sauce over. Sprinkle with cheese and bake at 375°F until bubbling and golden. Serves six.

If you don't want to make fish stock, use ⅔ pint clam juice cut with ⅓ pint water, or white wine.

BAKED FISH, TROUT OR BASS

3 pounds sea trout or bass,
    dressed
salt and pepper
2 garlic cloves, minced
3 tablespoons chopped parsley
1 green pepper, sliced

¼ cup celery, chopped
2 carrots, sliced
2 onions, sliced
2 cups canned tomatoes
½ cup olive oil
½ cup water

Season the fish with salt and fresh ground pepper. Place garlic, parsley and all the vegetables except tomatoes in a shallow baking dish and season, then lay the fish over. Combine the tomatoes, water and olive oil and pour over the fish. Bake at 350°F for 1 hour. Serves six.

MOCK CRAB IMPERIAL (HADDOCK)

"It fools you," says Agnes Scott of her clever, money saving recipe. Substitute haddock totally, or use half crab meat.

1 cup water
1 teaspoon Old Bay seasoning
2 bay leaves
2 tablespoons lemon juice
salt to taste
1 pound haddock fillets
1 package cream cheese (8 ounces)
¼ cup mayonnaise

1 teaspoon dry mustard
½ teaspoon Worcestershire sauce
salt and pepper to taste
dash garlic salt
1 tablespoon grated Parmesan cheese
dash paprika

In a saucepan, bring to a boil the water, Old Bay seasoning, salt, lemon juice and bay leaves. Lay in the fish and simmer 10 to 12 minutes until the fish flakes easily. Drain, remove bay leaves and flake the fish with a fork.

Soften the cream cheese, then blend into it the mayonnaise, mustard, Worcestershire, salt, pepper and garlic salt. Fold the cooked fish into the mixture, then turn into a shallow baking dish. Sprinkle with Parmesan and paprika and broil until brown and bubbly. Serves four.

POACHED SALMON I

Expensive—but oh, so good on a summer night. Visually the pink salmon is a delight, and the flavor is delicate. If you make it, try serving cucumbers, French bread and a very dry white wine, ice cold, with it.

3-pound center-cut piece of fresh salmon	2 sprigs parsley
2 quarts water	pinch of thyme
1½ cups dry white wine	6 peppercorns
1 onion, cut up	1 tablespoon salt

Put all ingredients into a large kettle except the salmon. Simmer 30 minutes. (If you have a rack that will fit on the bottom, so much the better. If not, don't worry—we'll get it out in one piece.)

Wrap the salmon closely in cheesecloth and lower it into the pot. Bring the bouillon back to simmer, and very gently poach the salmon about 25 minutes. Let it cool in the liquid.

Lift out—the cheesecloth will hold it together—then unwrap. Chill thoroughly. Before serving remove the top side of any gray. The whole piece should be pink. Serve very cold with mayonnaise.

POACHED SALMON II

Without the wine or vegetables, the salmon still tastes wonderful because of its affinity for dill.

3 pound center-cut piece of fresh salmon	3 large sprigs fresh dill
3 quarts water	6 peppercorns
	skimpy tablespoon salt

Proceed exactly as in Recipe I.

SALMON LOAF

An old fashioned American recipe that's still a fine family meal. This is especially good with cucumbers on the side, marinated and chilled.

2 cans salmon (1 pound size)	1 small onion, grated
2 cups fresh whole wheat bread crumbs	1 can cream of celery soup (10¾ ounces)
2 eggs	2 lemons cut in wedges

Generously grease an 8½ x 4½ inch loaf pan. In a bowl, with a fork, combine the salmon, bread crumbs, eggs, onion and ⅓ cup of the celery soup. Press evenly into the pan, making sure the bottom corners are filled.

Bake in a 375°F oven for 50 to 55 minutes until a knife inserted in the center comes out clean.

Invert on a serving platter and serve with a sauce made by combining the remaining soup with ½ cup water and heating. Garnish with lemon wedges. Serves eight.

BAKED SHAD WITH ROE STUFFING

Every Spring, in our mid Atlantic area, a miracle happens. The shad runs, the asparagus pops up and in come the first splendid strawberries. It is a time for feasting. Here's a Maryland recipe for shad and roe fans that will delight you.

1 whole dressed shad and roe	1 cup soft bread crumbs
2 tablespoons chopped parsley	¼ pound melted butter
2 scant tablespoons grated onion	salt and pepper to taste
	good dry white wine

Scald the roe for 2 minutes. Drain it, then split and scrape out the roe. In a bowl, combine the roe with parsley, onion, bread crumbs and enough melted butter to soften the crumbs. Season. Pour on a little white wine, then stuff the fish. Tie it up or skewer it closed and put in a shallow buttered pan. Sprinkle lightly with flour, salt and pepper.

Bake at 325°F for about an hour. Baste the fish frequently with melted butter, adding a little more wine to the pan juices as it bakes. Serve garnished with parsley and lemon wedges. Serves six.

BAKED TROUT IN WHITE WINE

Served with dill over the rainbows!

6 frozen rainbow trout, thawed
2 tablespoons lemon juice
salt and pepper
1 cup dry white wine
2 tablespoons chopped fresh
    parsley
¼ cup finely sliced scallions

2 tablespoons fine dry bread
    crumbs
¼ cup melted butter or mar-
    garine
fresh or dry dill
6 thin lemon slices

Wash trout and pat dry. Brush the inside of each with some of the lemon juice and sprinkle with salt and pepper.

Pour wine into a shallow baking dish and sprinkle the onions and parsley evenly into it. Arrange the trout in the dish and sprinkle with the bread crumbs. Spoon melted butter over the crumbs and bake, uncovered, in a 400°F oven for 25 minutes, or until the fish flakes easily.

Serve on a heated platter garnished with dill and lemon wedges. Serves six.

TUNA MOUSSE

Remember when your favorite cheapie dinner was a tuna noodle casserole? Now, between the tuna wars and the inflation, the old kitchen standby is downright expensive. On the other hand, what isn't?

This easy-to-make mousse will delight eight ladies for lunch, or six of you for a summer supper. It's a handsome piece for any buffet.

2 envelopes unflavored gelatin	**2 cups finely diced celery**
1½ cups cold water	**⅔ cup sliced stuffed olives**
¼ cup lemon juice	**2 cans tuna, well drained**
1½ cups mayonnaise	**(7 ounce size)**

Put the cold water in a saucepan and sprinkle the gelatin over it to soften. Place over low heat, stirring all the while until the gelatin is dissolved. Take off the heat, stir in the lemon juice and cool.

Put the mayonnaise into a good sized bowl and gradually stir the gelatin mixture into it. Add the remaining ingredients, distributing evenly. Turn into a six cup mold, or eight individual molds and chill until firm. Unmold on greens.

Instead of using vegetable oil to prepare the molds, use a thin coating of mayonnaise.

Shellfish

CRAB IMPERIAL

½ stick butter or margarine
½ cup chopped onion
½ cup chopped green pepper
1 tablespoon prepared mustard
1 pound special or backfin crab
    meat

½ cup sherry
3 dashes Tabasco
1 cup mayonnaise
nutmeg
Parmesan cheese

Sauté onions and pepper in butter over low heat until tender but not brown. Stir in mustard. Add crab meat, sherry and Tabasco and mix well without shredding the crab meat.

Add the mayonnaise and turn the mixture into a small buttered casserole or three or four individual baking shells. Sprinkle lightly with nutmeg, then with cheese. Brown carefully under the broiler. Serves three to four.

CRAB IMPERIAL DE LUXE

A wonderful way for crabs to end up in Maryland.

2 pounds lump crab meat
½ cup mayonnaise
2 teaspoons lemon juice
3 whole pimentos, chopped
1 teaspoon salt

⅛ teaspoon pepper
¼ teaspoon dry mustard
2 more tablespoons mayonnaise
paprika

In a bowl, fork through crab meat carefully to remove any bits of shell but try not to break it up too much.

In a small bowl, combine the ½ cup mayonnaise with salt, lemon juice, pimento, pepper and mustard. Pour over the crab, and through it lightly, to mix.

Divide the mixture among six buttered ramekins or large shells. Smooth a little mayonnaise over the top of each and sprinkle with paprika. Bake at 350°F for 20 to 25 minutes until bubbly and lightly brown.

SOUTHERN CRAB MEAT

You can't get to the Lippincott's table when Frances serves this at a buffet. People just position themselves at the chafing dish and don't move. Just eat.

1 pound crab meat, preferably backfin	½ pint light cream
4 tablespoons butter	4 tablespoons sherry
4 tablespoons flour	salt, pepper to taste

Make a cream sauce with the butter, flour and cream. Season with salt, pepper and sherry. Take off the heat and gently stir in the lump crab meat.

Serve in a chafing dish with Melba toast, or serve in a casserole as a main dish, or serve over mushrooms lining a well buttered baking dish, baked at 350°F for 10 minutes.

How many? For the cocktail buffet, it depends on how many other dishes are there. The plain casserole will serve four as an entree, the mushroom one, six.

CRAB CUTLET

Always use the best crab you can afford, but for the cutlets, or cakes, special grade will do just fine. Harder to pick over, it still has fine flavor.

1 pound crab meat	1 teaspoon salt
1 cup thick cream sauce	pinch red pepper
1 tablespoon chopped parsley	1 egg
1 tablespoon finely chopped pimento	1 tablespoon milk
	fine bread crumbs

Mix the crab meat (well picked over) with the sauce and seasonings gently so as not to break up the crab too much. Refrigerate the mixture until quite cold.

Form into cutlets, oval, or cakes, round, shaping with floured hands. Beat the egg with the tablespoon of milk, then dip each cutlet into egg, then bread crumbs. Make sure they are well covered.

Fry in deep hot fat, and drain by standing in a colander set on a pie plate—or if you want to be conventional, on several thicknesses of paper towels. Serve on a hot platter. Makes four large cutlets or six cakes.

OPEN FACE CRAB MEAT AND CHEESE SANDWICH

At the elegant Hotel DuPont in Wilmington, Delaware, this is never taken off the menu. Never.

Crab Mixture:

1 pound backfin crab meat
dash of Tabasco
1 teaspoon Worcestershire
  sauce

1 teaspoon lemon juice
¼ cup mayonnaise

Pick over the crab meat carefully, then combine with mayonnaise, lemon juice, Worcestershire and Tabasco.

The Sandwich:

10 slices toast, crust on
5 tablespoons tartar sauce

10 slices American cheese
paprika

Spread five slices of toast with tartar sauce, then the crab mixture. Top each with two cheese slices. Dash the cheese with paprika, then run under the broiler until bubbling.

Serve with toast points made by halving the other five pieces of toast. Serves five.

COQUILLES ST. JACQUES
(Scallops in Sauce)

In the average restaurant, I have found myself spearing around a bowl of white sauce hunting for a few scallops. That's not the way this dish should be. This delicate interpretation will serve four as a main course, six for luncheon and eight as a first course.

The Scallops:

1½ pounds bay or sea scallops	8 peppercorns
¼ teaspoon thyme	salt
half a bay leaf	½ cup dry white wine
2 sprigs parsley	½ cup water

Put bay scallops, or thinly sliced sea scallops into a small saucepan with the wine, water, peppercorns and salt, parsley, bay leaf and thyme. Cover and simmer just 2 minutes. Drain, reserving the scallop liquid.

The Sauce:

7 tablespoons butter	1 teaspoon lemon juice
3 tablespoons flour	cayenne pepper
2 egg yolks	grated Gruyère cheese

Melt 2 tablespoons of the butter in a saucepan and stir in the flour. Cook the roux 1 or 2 minutes then stir in 1½ cups of the scallop liquid. (Add water to make up the 1½ cups, if necessary.) Stir constantly as the sauce cooks, blends and thickens.

Remove from the heat and with a rotary beater or your hand mixer, beat the sauce as you add the remaining 5 tablespoons butter, a little at a time, the egg yolks, lemon juice and cayenne. Continue beating until the sauce is somewhat cooled.

Using scallop shells, ramekins or shirred egg dishes, spoon a little sauce into the bottom of each. Divide the cooked scallops among the dishes, then cover with the remaining sauce. Sprinkle with Gruyère cheese and bake in a 400°F oven for 5 to 10 minutes until the top bubbles and turns gold. Do not overcook. If the top isn't brown enough to suit you, run briefly under the broiler.

SCALLOPS WITH BACON

1 pound sea scallops in 16 pieces
5 ounces melted butter
8 slices bacon, cut in half
¾ cup fine fresh white bread
    crumbs

4 tablespoons chopped parsley
    seasoned with black pepper

Dry scallops and cut to 16 bite size pieces. Dip in melted butter then roll in the bread crumbs you have mixed with the parsley and pepper.

Wrap a piece of bacon around each scallop and thread on skewers. Broil till bacon is crisp. Serve with melted butter and lemon wedges.

SCALLOPS IN PROSCIUTTO

These scallop hors d' oeuvres are very classy indeed. Use bay scallops whole or cut sea scallops into bite sizes.

24 bay scallops or 24 pieces of
   sea scallops
24 slices prosciutto ham, small,
   paper thin

butter
buttered toast points
chopped parsley

Wrap each scallop in a small piece of prosciutto. Sauté in butter until the scallops are tender, about 15 to 20 minutes over low heat. Serve on buttered toast points with a sprinkle of parsley.

OYSTERS CASINO

These goodies can be speared as appetizers, or arrive in quantity as an entree. A Maryland speciality

6 slices bacon, cut in small
   pieces
2 little onions, finely chopped
2 small stalks celery, minced
2 tablespoons lemon juice
1½ teaspoons salt

¼ teaspoon pepper
12 drops Worcestershire sauce
8 drops hot sauce
½ teaspoon Old Bay seasoning
1 quart oysters, well drained

Fry bacon bits till crisp. Remove and set aside.

In the bacon drippings, sauté the onion and celery until tender. Add lemon juice and seasonings.

Arrange the drained oysters in a single layer in a shallow well buttered baking dish. Spread the onions and celery over, then sprinkle with the bacon bits.

Bake at 400°F for 10 minutes or less—not more. Serves four.

OYSTER AND WILD RICE CASSEROLE

A reader called one day to tell me she had made two of these casseroles for her daughter's wedding reception. See, 'tis better to cook than to throw!

2 cups wild rice	1 cup light cream
¼ pound butter	1 tablespoon finely chopped
2 pints small oysters	onion
salt and pepper to taste	½ teaspoon thyme
1 can cream of celery soup	minced parsley for garnish
(10¾ ounces)	

Cook the rice according to package directions. If you use white and wild mixed, don't use the seasonings from the box. If there is some liquid left when the rice is done, drain well. Cut up the butter and stir it into the rice.

Butter a large rather shallow baking dish, and spread the rice evenly over the bottom. Arrange the well drained oysters over the rice and sprinkle with salt and pepper. Heat the soup and cream together, seasoning with onion and thyme. Pour the hot soup mixture over the oysters, covering them up.

Bake in a slow, 300°F oven for 40 or 45 minutes. Serve sprinkled with chopped parsley. Serves twelve.

SCALLOPED OYSTERS

Almost all oyster casserole recipes call for cracker crumbs. While I have nothing against crackers, per se, the buttered toast crumbs in this recipe will give you a different texture and more flavor.

2 cups coarse toast crumbs
¼ cup melted butter
2 dozen oysters, drained
¼ cup oyster liquid
½ teaspoon salt
dash pepper

2 tablespoons light cream
1 teaspoon Worcestershire
    sauce
dash cayenne pepper
2 tablespoons sherry

Combine crumbs with the melted butter. Cover the bottom of a greased 10 x 6 x 2 inch baking dish with one third of the crumbs. Lay half the oysters over.

In a small bowl, combine the oyster liquid with salt, pepper, cream, Worcestershire, cayenne and sherry. Spoon half of this sauce over the oysters.

Sprinkle with the second third of the crumbs, another layer of the rest of the oysters then sauce, and a top layer of crumbs. Bake for 30 minutes at 425°F. Serves four.

HELEN'S LOBSTER DISH

Never tasted anything better, or made anything simpler than . . .

2 large rock lobster tails

Cook lobster until tender. Remove meat from the shells and set aside.

The Sauce:

1½ tablespoons butter
1½ tablespoons flour
1 cup light cream
3 tablespoons ketchup
¾ tablespoon Worcestershire
   sauce

½ teaspoon dry mustard
2 tablespoons dry sherry
salt, pepper to taste
dash of cayenne pepper

Melt the butter in a saucepan, add flour, and cook the roux gently for a few minutes. Add light cream and all other ingredients and cook, stirring, until a smooth, rich coral colored sauce is achieved.

Cut the lobster into large bite sized pieces. Add to the sauce. Keep hot as long as you like over hot water in a double boiler top. Serve over canned crisp Chinese noodles.

You can serve it over rice but it's not the same. The noodles are better. Serves three to four.

HELENE'S SHRIMP DISH

When the girls come for lunch, here's a delightful (and easy) dish you can put together in minutes just before the rice is done. Have everything all set, soup opened, liquids measured, shrimp and crab drained on a tray in the refrigerator and combine when you're ready.

1 can shrimp soup (10¾ ounces)
2 cans tiny shrimp (6½ ounce
   size)
⅔ cup light cream

½ to 1 cup dry sherry
1 can crab meat (6½ ounces)
1 tablespoon lemon juice

Combine soup, shrimp, cream and sherry in a saucepan and heat just to the boiling point. Start with ½ cup sherry then add to taste and thickness desired.

Add crab meat and lemon juice and serve over curried or saffron rice. Serves four to six.

SHRIMP ALMONDINE

From my favorite Southern belle, a party casserole that will please everyone's palate. This holds well. If the party is going great, turn off the oven and cover for 15 or 20 extra minutes.

[handwritten: ⅛ tsp pepper]

[handwritten: 2 ½] 2 pounds fresh shrimp, cooked, peeled
[handwritten: or 1 cup cooked precooked] ¾ cup regular rice cooked in 1 cup water
[handwritten: 2] 4 tablespoons butter
¼ cup chopped green pepper
¼ cup chopped green onion
1 teaspoon salt

⅛ teaspoon mace
1 can tomato soup (10¾ ounces)
1 cup light cream (or half and half) *[handwritten: Heavy]*
½ cup sherry (dry)
[handwritten: ¼] ½ cup slivered almonds
paprika

[handwritten: Sauté - pepper + onion]
[handwritten: Put together a little differently!]

Stir the 4 tablespoons of butter into the hot cooked rice then put everything together. Mix well and sprinkle with paprika. Bake at 350°F for 45 minutes. Serves ten to twelve.

You know what's good with this? Orange and sliced onion salad with Fruity French Dressing.

SHRIMP CHOW MEIN

The supermarket version is a pale imitation of this famous Chinese American dish. Please note that it is better made a day ahead. This is from Vivian Rash who says, "I never can wait twenty four hours so I usually make it up only a few hours before eating!"

1 pound shrimp, cooked, peeled, diced in chunks
¼ cup shortening, bacon drippings preferred
1 heaping cup chopped onions
1 teaspoon salt
⅛ teaspoon pepper

1 heaping cup celery pieces, cut diagonally every half inch of the stalk
1 can bean sprouts, drained, reserve liquid
1 can mushroom pieces, drained, reserve liquid

Pause here. Add enough water to the drained vegetable liquid to make 1¼ cups of liquid. Use ¾ cup vegetable liquid with the shrimp mixture, reserve the rest.

Melt the shortening in a large skillet, add the onions and sauté, stirring the first few minutes then cooking with the lid on for 5 minutes. Add the celery, salt, pepper and vegetable liquid (¾ cup). Mix, cover and cook another 5 minutes.

Add bean sprouts, shrimp and mushrooms, mix and bring to the boiling point. Stir in thickening (see below), cover and cook for 5 more minutes. Cool and refrigerate for twenty four hours.

Reheat before serving, piping hot, over chow mein noodles or plain rice. Serve soy sauce on the side. Serves two to three.

The Thickening:

½ cup vegetable water liquid	1 tablespoon soy sauce
2 tablespoons cornstarch	1 tablespoon molasses

Mix together well, stirring until the cornstarch is dissolved.

As in almost all Chinese oriented dishes, the work comes before the cooking. If you have the vegetables cut up, the shrimp cooked and cut up, the thickening ready, the actual cooking time is under 20 minutes.

SHRIMP AND ASPARAGUS ROLLS

When you have the girls for lunch, they'll want the recipe, I assure you. Please note that for once, you use our much maligned ordinary white sandwich bread. It rolls out better.

12 slices plain white bread
2 cans small shrimp (5 ounce size)
¼ teaspoon Worcestershire sauce
dash Tabasco
2 teaspoons horseradish sauce

½ cup mayonnaise
12 cooked asparagus spears (fat)
melted butter
paprika
mushroom sauce

Trim crusts from bread and roll out the slices with a rolling pin until quite thin and elastic. Mash shrimp with Tabasco, Worcestershire, horseradish and mayonnaise. Spread evenly on the bread slices.

Lay one plump asparagus spear on each slice, trimming the stalk if necessary. Roll up and secure with toothpicks. Brush generously with melted butter and sprinkle with paprika.

Arrange on an ungreased baking sheet, and bake at 450°F until golden brown, about 15 minutes. Check at 10 minutes. Remove picks and serve with mushroom sauce. Probably two each for luncheon, three for an entree.

SHRIMP FONDUE

Not a dip it fondue but an oven puffed, shrimp rich casserole that lets a pound of shrimp feed eight.

6 slices white bread
butter
1 pound cooked shrimp, bite size
2 cups grated American cheese
salt and pepper

3 eggs, slightly beaten
2 cups milk
½ teaspoon Worcestershire sauce

Cut the crusts from the bread, butter liberally, then cut into half inch cubes. Spread a third of the cubes in the bottom of a greased, medium sized casserole. Top with a third of the shrimp, a third of the cheese, sprinkling with a little salt and pepper. Repeat with the rest of the bread, shrimp and cheese.

Beat together the eggs, milk and Worcestershire and pour over the whole. Set in a pan of hot water and bake at 350°F for 1 hour and 15 minutes. Serves eight.

SHRIMP AU GRATIN

A very rich and delicious casserole which will serve four with only one pound of shrimp.

1 pound medium shrimp, cooked, cleaned
3 tablespoons butter
3 tablespoons flour
1 cup evaporated milk
½ cup water

1 heaping teaspoon paprika
1½ cups grated sharp Cheddar cheese
4 slices white bread, cubed
3 tablespoons melted butter
grated Parmesan cheese

Arrange the shrimp on the bottom of a 1½ to 2-quart casserole.

In a saucepan, melt the butter, add the flour, then gently cook the roux over low heat a minute or so. Add the milk and water and cook, stirring, until the sauce is thickened. Add paprika and cheese and stir until the cheese is melted. Pour the sauce over the shrimp.

Toss the bread cubes in the melted butter then strew evenly over the sauce. Sprinkle with Parmesan and bake for 20 minutes in a 400°F oven.

SHRIMP VILLA MONTANA

Lois Budd sent this all the way from Mexico, an admirable export. This makes an exceptional buffet dish.

6 deviled eggs (12 halves)
½ pound fresh mushrooms, sliced
1½ pounds cooked, peeled shrimp, medium size or cut into bite size pieces

3 slices white bread, diced, browned in butter

Devil the eggs and arrange in the bottom of a buttered shallow baking dish. Sauté the mushroom slices in butter and lay them over the eggs. Arrange the shrimp pieces over the mushrooms.

The Sauce:

4 tablespoons butter
4 tablespoons flour
2½ cups milk

½ to 1 cup grated American cheese to taste
salt and pepper

Melt the butter, add the flour, cook for 1 or 2 minutes. Heat the milk slightly and add to the roux. Cook until thickened. Season with salt and pepper, then add the cheese to your liking.

Pour sauce over the shrimp, top with browned croutons, and bake in a 350°F oven for about 30 minutes. Serves six.

Kitchen Chemistry

When I was a junior at the McKeesport, Pennsylvania senior high school, I was forced to take Chemistry I for a whole terrible year. It was required for college preparatory, although I was planning to major in music.

The only reason I got a miserable C in the course (of which I remember only the smell of sulphur and several nasty burns) was because Mr. Dodd, the teacher, was devoted to music, especially the 1812 Overture, and regarded me with some esteem because I played the piano well.

When I look back on all this, I wonder why they didn't teach me the chemistry of cooking. What a fascinating, useful course that would have been!

Instead of aimless experiments which were mere exercises, I might have learned why yeast makes bread rise, and what makes cream puff dough come suddenly away from the pan.

They might have taught me, not how to volatilize some smelly liquid over a Bunsen burner, but how to cook down a liquid into a sauce, and why wine evaporates but leaves its flavor.

Why do tomatoes and peaches ruin the pan? Why does a drop of water in hot fat make a stinging splash? What happens when the egg performs its countless wonders?

What's in baking powder? Why does soda want sour milk instead of sweet?

How interesting it would have been to learn these marvelously useful things. How interesting, indeed, it would be today.

Instead of cooking by rote, learning from repetitive experience, we'd really know why we do the things we do. We could read a label and know good or harm was contained inside.

I am not talking about a cooking course per se, but a real chemistry course using mayonnaise instead of potassium and a range instead of a burner, casseroles instead of retorts.

When I consider the hours I have spent in cookery opposed to the number of times I have need to know that H_2O is water and NaCl is salt (I think), it's pretty ludicrous.

Maybe sometime, a forward looking school will be creative enough to give girls and boys a whack at the future with a Chemistry of Cooking course.

It would stand them in good stead.

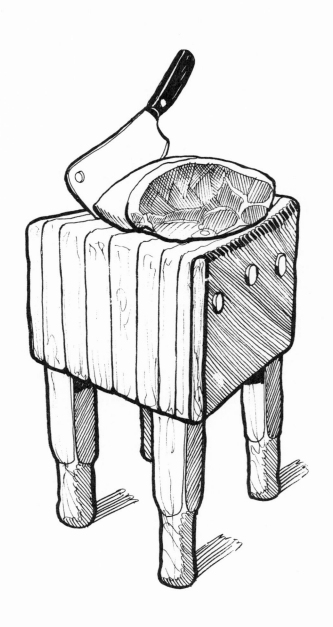

A Meaty Subject...

Beef, Pork, Ham, Sausage, Veal, Lamb

When America was young, we were not a nation of carnivores.

The early settlers shot fowl and game, but raised stock for breeding. It was not until later that we became the big meat eaters, not until the railroads were able to ship beef from shore to shore, and then we really went at it.

Beef, that's our thing, and we consume about one hundred pounds a year per person. No wonder. Outside of a few unusual and very expensive foreign beefs like the French Charolais or the Japanese super beef that costs about $20 a pound, we have the tenderest, best beef in the world.

Along the way, we kind of forgot about veal, highly regarded in other cuisines, eating only three pounds per person, per annum. We consume just two pounds of lamb, but tuck away a hefty fifty-four pounds of pork—of course, that includes our breakfast bacon and sausage.

These figures are from a 1976 release by the Department of Agriculture, and have probably changed somewhat due to inflation. That year we ate forty-three pounds of chicken each, but I would presume that each passing year we will lower the pork, and up the chicken figure.

At any rate, when you do get hold of good meat, cook it well, and try not to think of how much it cost per bite. For roasting, use a meat thermometer, no matter how skillful a cook you are.

When you broil beef, keep it a good five inches from gas or charcoal, but only three inches from electric heat. To make sure it's the way you want it, poke it with your finger. If it's spongy it's raw inside. If just medium rare, it will be firm but give a little. Of course, if it's hard, you've blown it.

When you braise meat, do it in a pan that the meat fits closely in. Covered, it will steam the meat if there is too much liquid around. When you braise, vegetables are added to flavor the dish but they are minced, serve as a bed, and in the end are puréed into the sauce.

If you stew meat, the liquid may be much more plentiful, the vegetables bite size. When you stew white meat, veal or chicken, use white vegetables to make a true blanquette, onions, potatoes, turnips etc.

Deep frying is the trickiest meat operation because even when you use a thermometer or have an electric fryer with a thermostat, every time you drop a piece of meat in, the temperature changes. (To deflavor oil, fry a heel of bread for 5 minutes.)

For sautéing, broiling or frying, always bring the meat to room temperature. I do that with a big roast as well, otherwise it affects the roasting time.

Whatever your desires, the probability is that we're all going to be eating less meat in the future. In the end, we will benefit, avoiding all that delicious flavorful fat.

But you're going to have to be inventive, to make a little go a long way, or to spend more time cooking the less expensive, slow cooking meats.

Sausage, especially sweet Italian, is great to use with other foods in a casserole. I have even seen a recipe for lasagna that used sausage and chicken instead of expensive beef.

Try Polish keilbasa with sauerkraut instead of pork. Chicken livers are still inexpensive, and can be the basis for many good dishes. Substitute veal tenders for cutlet, and find recipes that use ground or cubed veal which is not as dear.

While ham is high, you can get so many meals out of a ham that you might want to figure that one out, dollar wise. Slices off, butt end for soup, thin slices for Eggs Benedict, and the bulk to bake. Sandwiches later. It's still a good investment.

You'll find next a number of extended meat dishes, using vegetables to make them go farther, and a comparable number of economical recipes under Pasta.

Beef

CARBONNADES OF BEEF

Men love this big, rich and flavorful dish which had its origins in the Flemish part of Belgium. While there are many interpretations, each one has beef, lots of onions, beer and some sweet and sour touch. I serve this with small boiled potatoes, applesauce and, of course, ice cold beer.

3 pounds lean beef chuck cubes
vegetable oil
salt and pepper
6 tablespoons butter
6 cups thinly sliced onions
3 tablespoons flour
2 cups beer

1 cup beef stock
1 tablespoon wine vinegar
1 tablespoon brown sugar
1 large clove garlic, minced
2 sprigs parsley, 1 bay leaf tied
   together
pinch thyme

Brown the beef cubes in vegetable oil in the Dutch oven, seasoning with salt and pepper. You may do better in two batches, browning well on all sides. Remove the cubes and set aside.

Add butter to the pan and gently cook the onions, stirring occasionally until they are tender and golden. Sprinkle the flour over the onions, mix well, then pour in the beer and the beef broth. Stir in the vinegar, brown sugar and garlic. Return the meat to the pan and put in the parsley, bay leaf garni and thyme.

Cook over low heat on top of the stove, or in a 325°F oven for about 2 hours. The meat should be fork-tender and the onions completely gone to sauce. Serves six, or if you put it over noodles, eight.

VIENNESE BOILED BEEF WITH HORSERADISH SAUCE

If you tell someone you boil beef, they have a fit! But this famous dish, which had Viennese origins, is exceptionally good and liked especially by men. Just don't mention that it's boiled. He'll never know.

3 pounds lean brisket, first cut
boiling water
3 leeks, trimmed and well
   washed
1 bay leaf
1 whole carrot peeled

1 medium onion, peeled and
   whole
1 small stalk celery with leaves
salt to taste
1 dozen peppercorns
   cracked

Place the brisket in your Dutch oven and pour boiling water over it. Bring back to boil until the scum arises, then pour off the water and cover with fresh. This is faster than ladling off the grease and bits that surface.

Add all the remaining ingredients, cover and simmer for 3 to 4 hours until the meat is fork tender.

Horseradish Sauce:

1½ cups beef broth
3 tablespoons butter

3 tablespoons flour
horseradish to taste

Without removing the meat from the pan, ladle out a cup and a half of the broth and set aside. This should leave enough liquid in the pan so that you can keep the meat hot.

Melt the butter in a small saucepan, add the flour to make a roux, cook briefly then gradually add the hot beef stock. Stir until it is thick and smooth. Remove from heat and stir in horseradish to taste, starting with 2 tablespoons and adding more if you like.

To serve, slice the meat very thin against the grain, on the diagonal the way you slice flank steak. Cover the slices on each plate with the sauce.

Boiled new potatoes, applesauce or coleslaw, any green vegetable and cold beer go well with this.

 To make the sauce smoother, put a small strainer over the two cup measure and ladle the broth through it when you take it from the pan.

CORNED BEEF WITH ORANGES

The only thing comparable to the pleasure of having a cooked ham in the refrigerator is having a piece of corned beef ready for slicing. While this is a hot entree, be sure to put some back for sandwiches.

1 corned beef brisket
2 oranges, sliced
1 lemon sliced
1 large onion, sliced
¼ cup brown sugar
   packed

1 tablespoon pickling spices
additional brown sugar for
   baking

Cover the brisket with cold water in a heavy kettle, and add everything else except the extra brown sugar. Simmer and bubble it about 4 hours or until tender. (Check package instructions to be sure.) You can do this in the morning or a day ahead if you want.

When the brisket is very tender, remove it from the liquid, sprinkle with the brown sugar and bake in a 350°F oven until the sugar is melted and glazed.

Slice very thin and arrange on a platter garnished with orange slices.

 If you prefer corned beef in the ordinary way, try serving it some night with spoon bread and, of course, some spicy mustard. It makes a good combination.

STUFFED CABBAGE

When I was growing up in a small town, the only swimming oppor-
tunities we had in the winter were on Tuesdays after school and
early evening. Then the YMCA closed their pool to the boys and let
us girls enjoy it. We would go right after school, stay to the last
minute then walk home, six or seven of us in the winter night,
arriving home long after dinner was over.

When my Mother had stuffed cabbage, kept hot for me in the oven, it
tasted absolutely wonderful. The ferocious appetite developed by
swimming and the long walk might explain it in part, but this is one
of my favorite peasanty dishes. I looked for years for a recipe as good
as Mother's, and this is it. Forgive me, Mother—it might even be a
little bit better.

1 large cabbage	4 tablespoons chopped parsley
⅓ cup uncooked rice, regular or minute	6 slices bacon, cut in squares (1 inch)
1 egg, slightly beaten	1 can tomatoes (16 ounces)
¾ pound ground beef	1 can tomato sauce (8 ounces)
½ cup chopped onion	1 bay leaf
1 teaspoon salt	sour cream
few grinds of pepper	

Cook the rice according to package directions. Mix it in a bowl
with the meat, egg, ¼ cup onions, salt and pepper, and parsley.

Discard any spoiled cabbage leaves, cut away the heavy core,
then pull off eight big outer leaves of the cabbage. Parboil
them in water just to cover—a few minutes will do it. To make
the leaves easier to shape, cut a vee in each where the heavy
stem is. If the cabbage is very elderly, you might want to cut
away some of the white vein on the leaf's outside.

While the leaves parboil, chop the best of the rest of the
cabbage and use it to make a bed in a baking dish, shallow
and large enough to hold the eight rolls.

Remove the leaves, drain and divide the meat mixture among
them. Roll each into a tidy package and put, seam side down,
on the cabbage in the baking dish.

To make the sauce: Sauté the bacon squares, add the remaining ¼ cup onion and cook till tender. Add tomatoes, tomato sauce and the bay leaf. Simmer 5 minutes or more, then pour over the rolls. Bake them 90 minutes at 350°F, covering the last ½ hour to keep them from browning.

Serve the rolls and the cooked cabbage with a bowl of sour cream alongside. Serves eight.

SWEET AND SOUR BEEF

A sturdy dish which is perfectly simple and only wants a little minding. Set the timer for one hour. Set the timer for another hour. Set the timer for a half hour. Dinner's ready!

3 pound piece of boneless chuck
    roast
vegetable oil
2 large onions, sliced
1 garlic clove, minced
¾ cup beef stock
2 bay leaves

2 tablespoons lemon juice
1 tablespoon brown sugar
    (rounded)
3 tablespoons ketchup
¼ cup raisins
salt and pepper to taste

Brown the meat in vegetable oil in a Dutch oven, season with salt and pepper. Add onions and garlic, saute briefly, then add the beef stock and bay leaves. Simmer, covered for 1 hour.

Add lemon juice and sugar and simmer, covered, for another hour.

Finally, add raisins and ketchup and simmer for the last 30 minutes. Serves six, sliced thin with the sauce over good noodles.

SUKIYAKI

A ready, get set, go recipe. If you have everything set, it won't take more than twelve minutes to cook.

1½ pounds steak, sliced paper
    thin, in small pieces
¼ cup vegetable oil
½ cup bouillon
½ cup soy sauce
1 tablespoon sugar
1 tablespoon dry sherry

3 medium onions, sliced thin
1 cup celery, sliced thin
1 cup bamboo shoots, sliced
½ pound mushrooms, sliced
1 cup fresh spinach, stemmed
4 scallions, sliced

Prepare the vegetables. Make a sauce by combining the oil, bouillon, soy sauce, sugar and sherry.

In a good hot skillet, quickly brown the meat. Reduce heat somewhat and add half the soy sauce mixture. Push the meat aside, add the onions and celery and cook on low heat just 3 minutes. Add the rest of the soy sauce mixture, then the bamboo shoots, mushrooms and spinach and cook 3 minutes more. Put in the green onions and cook for 1 minute.

Serves four to six over Chinese noodles or rice.

STEAK IN A BAG

Do you think you would like a delicious medium rare steak with a really well seasoned crust around it? Try this unusual treatment. The weight of the steak can vary.

2 inch thick sirloin steak
4 tablespoons olive oil
2 tablespoons salt
4 teaspoons cracked pepper

1½ cloves garlic, minced
1 package Pepperidge Farm
    stuffing mix

Combine olive oil, salt, pepper and garlic and spread it on both sides of the steak. Use it all. Now press the stuffing mix onto the steak to coat it completely. Bake, enclosed in a brown paper bag at 375°F for 35 to 40 minutes for medium rare. Slice and serve.

A note of caution: paper will char and even blaze at 450°F. It is perfectly safe at the 375°F temperature in the recipe. However, if your oven is grossly inaccurate, use discretion.

 If you slit the bag the long way, you can do the coating right in the bag. Seal up and bake as above.

JOHNSON BROILED FLANK STEAK

This isn't gilding the lily—it's gilding the flank steak into a memorable taste.

1 flank steak, 1½ to 2 pounds
meat tenderizer

The gilding:

½ cup grated Parmesan cheese
1 teaspoon prepared mustard

½ teaspoon Worcestershire sauce

Mix cheese, mustard and Worcestershire together in a bowl. Set aside.

Sprinkle instant meat tenderizer on one side of the steak. Turn over and make a series of shallow diagonal cuts on the other side—about 1 inch apart. Place cut side down on the broiler rack and broil for 3 minutes.

Turn the steak and broil 3 minutes more. Slide out the broiler pan, spread the cheese mixture over the steak, pressing it down into the cuts. Broil 2 more minutes. Slice very thin on the diagonal and serve to four to six.

NANCY'S BEEF RAGOUT

A sturdy casserole that's better made a day ahead. If you do this, don't add the dill and sour cream until just before serving.

3 pounds lean beef chuck in two
    inch cubes
3 tablespoons butter
2 tablespoons cooking oil
salt and fresh ground pepper
3 large onions, minced
2 garlic cloves, finely minced
1 teaspoon good paprika
2 tablespoons tomato paste

½ teaspoon marjoram
½ teaspoon thyme
2 cups peeled sliced carrots
beef stock or broth
2 tablespoons chopped fresh
    dill or 1 tablespoon dill
    weed, dried
1 cup sour cream

In your Dutch oven, heat the butter and oil and brown the beef cubes in several batches, seasoning with salt and pepper as you go. Remove as you brown and set aside.

Add onions and garlic to the pan and cook until tender, not browned—you may need more oil. Add the paprika, tomato paste, marjoram and thyme and mix.

Return the meat to the pan, stirring it into the onions, then add the sliced carrots and about ½ cup beef stock. Cover the pan and cook for 2 hours in a 350°F oven. Check occasionally to make sure there is liquid. If not, add a little more stock.

Remove from the oven and taste for seasoning. Mix the chopped or dried dill into the sour cream, and fold into the ragout. Serves six to eight.

BEEF STEFADO

A simple beef stew with a Greek accent—or is it an onion stew?

6 tablespoons olive oil
2 pounds lean beef chuck in 2-
    inch cubes
3 tablespoons tomato paste
½ cup dry red wine

2 garlic cloves
2 bay leaves
¼ cup water
2 pounds small white onions
salt and pepper to taste

Brown the beef cubes on all sides in the olive oil. Add all ingredients except the onions. Simmer for 20 minutes, then add the onions, cover and cook for 2 hours until the meat is tender. Serves five to six. Good with plain rice.

SWEET AND SOUR MEAT LOAF

Where is the family that doesn't like meat loaf? Not in the U.S.A., and not in France with its good country pâtés, just other sorts of meat loaves. Funny, it always sounds fancier in French! This has a good zingy flavor.

1 can tomato sauce (8 ounces)
¼ cup brown sugar
¼ cup vinegar
1 teaspoon prepared mustard
1 egg, beaten

1 medium onion, minced
¼ cup crushed crackers
2 pounds ground lean chuck
1 teaspoon salt
a few grinds of pepper

Mix the tomato sauce with sugar, vinegar and mustard. In a bowl, combine egg, onions, cracker crumbs, meat, salt and pepper with just half the tomato sauce. (If you have an extra minute, sauté the onions briefly in a little butter before adding them.)

Shape the meat mixture into a loaf, and bake at 375°F for 1 hour. Reheat the remaining sauce and serve on the side. Serves six.

GREEN BEAN MOUSSAKA

This may be the only recipe in the world that substitutes green beans for pasta. The outcome is a fine dish for your family or informal entertaining.

1 can green beans, drained (16 ounces)
1½ pounds ground beef
1 can tomato sauce (8 ounces)
½ teaspoon salt
dash of cinnamon

1½ cups ricotta or creamy cottage cheese
2 slightly beaten eggs
1 teaspoon chopped chives
grated Parmesan cheese

Drain beans and arrange in the bottom of a 1½ quart casserole.

In a skillet, sauté the beef till nicely browned, then drain off the fat. Add tomato sauce, salt and cinammon. Simmer for 5 minutes then spread the meat mixture over the waiting beans.

In a bowl, mix together the riccota and the slightly beaten eggs, add the chives and layer this mixture over the meat. Sprinkle the top with the Parmesan cheese and bake, uncovered for 30 minutes in a 350°F oven.

Pork

PORK BRAISED WITH BOURBON

For an important meal, a delectable and rich pork loin, easy to carve and serve.

3 pounds pork loin, boned and tied
½ cup Dijon mustard
⅔ cup dark brown sugar
2 tablespoons peanut oil

⅔ cup bourbon whiskey
½ cup bouillon
salt and pepper
garnish of thyme, sage and parsley

Spread the mustard all over the pork loin, then roll it in brown sugar, pressing to make the sugar adhere evenly.

In your Dutch oven, brown the loin evenly in the oil. Keep the heat medium low because the sugar will caramelize, and if the heat is high, it will burn and alter the flavor.

When the meat is beautifully browned, very carefully pour over half the whiskey and flame it. The sugar is very hot and very flammable, and the flames will be high. Make sure you do this in a safe place and at a respectful distance.

When the flames die out, add the bouillon and cover the pan. Set in a 375°F oven to braise for 1 hour and 45 minutes. At the end of the first hour, turn the meat over and season with salt and pepper. Add the garnish, tied together.

Reduce the oven heat to 350°F and continue to braise for the remaining 45 minutes.

Remove the meat to a hot platter, strain the liquid and skim off the fat. (The easiest, fastest way to do this is to put the liquid in a tall narrow vessel like a glass. The fat comes to the top, deep enough for easy removal.)

Return the liquid to the pan, bring to a boil and add the remaining whiskey. Slice and serve the pork with this sauce on the side. Serves six.

BAKED PORK CHOPS WITH RICE

All in one supper that takes about five minutes to put together, then agreeably cooks itself in the oven for an hour.

4 large or 8 small pork chops
¾ cup brown rice
1½ cups chicken broth
2 medium onions, coarsely
    chopped
1 green pepper, coarsely
    chopped (optional)

¼ teaspoon of celery seed, or
    marjoram, or basil
1 teaspoon chopped parsley
salt and pepper

Brown the pork chops on both sides.

Put the rice in a lidded casserole, and arrange the chops on top. Sprinkle the onions and green pepper over, then pour in the broth. Season with salt and pepper and your choice of herbs.

Cover and bake for 1 hour at 350°F. Serves four.

 Frani likes spiced peaches or peach chutney with this.

THE HOUSE SAUERKRAUT

One New Year's Eve, I put the pork and sauerkraut on to roast while we went to an open house. That house was wide open. We stayed overlong. By the time we got home, I was certain all would be lost but voila! A Discovery!

Most of the liquid was gone but the top had turned to a golden brown and the flavor was indescribably good. Now we always overcook it and call it the House Sauerkraut.

5 pound pork loin roast
2 to 3 pounds sauerkraut
1 large onion, stuck with
  cloves

1 large apple, peeled, cored,
  quartered
2 garlic cloves
white wine, dry

Drain the sauerkraut in a colander and run water over it to rinse off some of the brine. Squeeze the rest out with your hands. (By removing the strong brine, you gentle the flavor so that even non-sauerkraut eaters may enjoy it. It also reduces the strength of the cooking aromas.)

In your Dutch oven, brown the roast on all sides. I generally have the butcher cut away the bone, then tie it back on the roast. You get the good flavor of the bone and later, when you remove it, the meat will slice more neatly.

Remove the browned roast and put the sauerkraut in the pan. In it, bury the onion, the apple and the garlic. Now pour over enough dry white wine to replace the liquid you removed.

Sprinkle the roast generously with salt and pepper—you can do this while you're browning if you prefer. Nestle the roast down in the kraut, cover and bake at 325°F for at least 3 hours. hours.

30 minutes before serving time, look at it. If the top is not golden and there is still a lot of liquid, cook the last half hour without the lid.

Serves eight. And they might like mashed buttery potatoes, cold applesauce and colder beer with it!

ANNE'S ORANGE GLAZED PORK

Roast me first, and glaze me later!

1 loin of pork, about 4 pounds
salt and pepper
1 small onion, grated
1 tablespoon butter
2 tablespoons brown sugar

1½ teaspoons cornstarch
½ teaspoon ground ginger
1 cup orange juice
1 tablespoon bottled steak sauce

Season the roast with salt and pepper and place fat side up on a rack in a roasting pan. Roast at 325°F for 90 minutes, or longer. Pork should be fall-off-the-bones tender.

While the pork roasts, make the glaze. Sauté the onion in the butter in a small saucepan a few minutes, add the brown sugar, then add the cornstarch you have dissolved in a little of the orange juice, the rest of the juice, the ginger and steak sauce. Cook until thickened and clear.

After 90 minutes of roasting, baste the pork with the glaze at 15 minute intervals for another hour in the oven. Carve and serve to six or eight, depending on how cleverly you carve.

Ham

CANADIAN BACON, CIDER GLAZED

Expensive, but extremely nice for a party brunch. This can be served hot or at room temperature.

3 pounds Canadian bacon in one
    piece
⅔ cup apple cider

⅔ cup light brown sugar
1 tablespoon cider vinegar
1 teaspoon dry mustard

Bake the bacon uncovered in a 350°F oven for 90 minutes, basting with cider every 15 minutes.

While the bacon bakes, combine the brown sugar, vinegar and mustard in a small bowl. After the meat has baked for the 90 minutes, spread the glaze over and bake for another 20 minutes. Cool a little before slicing thin and serving.

HAM LOAF WITH SAUCE

A nice change from the pineapple brown sugar syndrome.

1 cup white and wild rice mix
2 cups water
1 tablespoon butter
seasonings in the rice package
1½ pounds ground ham

1½ pounds ground pork
2 eggs, slightly beaten
½ can cream of tomato soup
   (10¾ ounce size)

Cook the rice according to package directions using the water, butter and seasonings.

Combine the meats, eggs, soup, and the cooked rice in a bowl and mix well. Shape into a loaf—it will be about 10 inches long—and bake uncovered in a shallow baking dish about 1 hour and 15 minutes. Serve with sweet and sour sauce or you might like this one:

Horseradish Sauce

1 cup heavy cream, whipped
   stiff
¼ cup horseradish

4 tablespoons Dijon mustard
1 teaspoon sugar

Fold this together, then taste for seasonings. Serve separately from the ham.

This recipe serves eight.

HAM IN CREAM SAUCE WITH SPINACH

Some years ago, I was traveling in France and en route specifically one day to Vienne, home of the then great Restaurant Pyramide. The most convenient stopover the night before was the town of Nevers, unattractive, in a station hotel equally unappealing.

You never know, do you? Asking for the specialty of the area, I was served this exceptional dish. They refused to give me the recipe, so for several years, I fooled around with it, always missing something. It was the port wine. I had been using dry wine, and that extra measure of flavor made all the difference. This can be done in the morning, reheated and served over the quick cooking spinach in just minutes.

(After all my efforts, the recipe showed up in Julia Child's first cook book, called Tranches de Jambon à la Crème!)

3 pounds precooked ham, sliced very thin	**2 tablespoons brandy**
2 tablespoons butter	**2 cups whipping cream**
2 tablespoons cooking oil	**2 tablespoons Dijon mustard mixed with**
2 tablespoons scallions, finely minced	**2 tablespoons tomato paste, and a little cream**
½ cup port wine	

The ham should be in serving size pieces. Brown the slices quickly in the hot oil and butter in a large heavy skillet. As you brown them, remove and set aside.

Pour most of the oil from the pan and sauté the scallions a few minutes, then pour in the wine and cognac and, scraping the skillet bottom, rapidly cook down the liquid until it barely covers the bottom of the pan.

Pour in the cream and add the mustard mixture. Cook slowly down until the cream has become a sauce, slightly thickened. Taste for seasoning, and do add a few grinds of pepper. The saltiness will depend on the ham.

Put the ham slices in the skillet, coating them with sauce. When ready to serve, cook and drain chopped or leaf spinach, and serve the ham slices and sauce right over. Serves six.

MRS. BEETON'S POTTED HAM

Mrs. Beeton was a redoubtable English lady who put together probably the first major comprehensive cook book in our language. If you make her potted ham—like our deviled ham—you will have an easier time than she with your blender or food processor. This is a real money saver, and you can freeze it.

2 pounds lean ham
1 tablespoon brown sugar
1 tablespoon prepared mustard
¼ pound margarine
1 teaspoon ground nutmeg

½ teaspoon ground allspice
2 tablespoons vinegar
dash cayenne pepper
2 tablespoons dried, minced onion

Cut the ham in small pieces, and in a big bowl, toss it with all other ingredients. Buzz or process as much as you can at a time. It should be smooth and spreadable. Pack in jars or plastic cups with tops and keep in the refrigerator for up to 2 weeks, or in the freezer for longer periods.

This is roughly the basic recipe but you may want, as I did, to spark it up a bit. Add more mustard to one little batch, horseradish to another. Combine some with sweet pickle relish and mayonnaise to make good sandwich spread.

Sausage

HUNT MEET SAUSAGE CHOWDER

A big dish for some big day when everyone comes in ravenous!

1 pound sausage meat
4 cups water
2 cans red kidney beans, drained (15¼ ounce size)
1 can tomatoes (1 pound, 13 ounces)
1 onion, chopped

1 bay leaf
½ garlic clove, minced
2 teaspoons salt
½ teaspoon thyme
dash of pepper
⅛ teaspoon caraway seed
pinch crushed red pepper

In a Dutch oven, brown the sausage meat, crumbling as you go. Drain off the fat and chop sausage finely.

Add all the rest of the ingredients and simmer for 1 hour, uncovered.

Now add:

1 cup diced raw potatoes
½ green pepper, chopped

Simmer, covered, for 20 more minutes. Serves eight to ten.

ITALIAN SAUSAGE CASSEROLE

Country style meal in a dish that is hearty and flavorful.

1½ pounds mild (sweet) Italian
    sausage
4 large potatoes, peeled, sliced
    thin
1 large onion, coarsely chopped
1 green pepper, coarsely
    chopped

salt and pepper
½ cup water
½ cup dry white wine
pinch or a few gratings of
    nutmeg

Put a little water in the bottom of a heavy skillet and simmer the sausage 5 to 10 minutes. Drain. Brown the sausage slowly and well.

Line the buttered bottom of a casserole that has a lid, with some of the potatoes. Sprinkle over some of the onion and green pepper. Repeat layers until the vegetables are used up, lightly salting as you go. Lay the sausage over the vegetables. Mix together the wine, water and nutmeg and pour over everything.

Bake with the lid on about 1 hour at 325°F, then remove the cover to let the sausage brown more. Serves four to six.

Veal

VEAL BALLS IN TOMATO SAUCE

To serve as an entree with pasta, or to be made very small to serve as hot hors d' oeuvres.

1 pound ground veal
½ pound mortadella or bologna, ground
¼ cup grated Parmesan or Romano cheese
2 eggs
2 teaspoons salt
¼ teaspoon fresh ground pepper
⅛ teaspoon nutmeg
½ cup flour
4 tablespoons olive oil
1 cup chopped onions
1 pound tomatoes, diced, or 1 medium can
2 tablespoons butter
1 garlic clove, minced

In a bowl, mix together the veal, mortadella, cheese, eggs, one teaspoon salt, the pepper and nutmeg. Shape in walnut size balls, roll in flour and put on a baking sheet to chill while you make the sauce.

Heat half the oil in a saucepan and sauté the onions until really tender. Add the tomatoes and the remaining teaspoon of salt. Season with pepper and cook over low heat for 30 minutes. Purée in the blender or processor.

Heat butter and remaining oil in a skillet and brown the veal balls. Don't crowd the skillet.

Add the garlic, and shake the pan as you sauté to keep the balls round. Finally, add the tomato sauce to the skillet and cook over low heat about 20 minutes. Serves four to six, more as an hors d' oeuvre.

VEAL BLANQUETTE

That should be Blanquette de Veau or else Veal Stew, but, although this is technically a stew, it is much too delicate and rich to end up as a stew. It uses veal cubes, which are probably the most economical pieces of veal to buy.

4 ounces butter
3 pounds veal in 1 to 1½ inch
   cubes
1 garlic clove, minced
½ cup onion, minced
salt and pepper
1 level tablespoon dill weed
⅓ cup flour

½ teaspoon nutmeg
1 cup chicken stock
1 cup water
2 carrots
2 leeks
3 ounces butter
¾ cup heavy cream
dill weed to taste

Heat the 4 ounces of butter in a fire-proof casserole or Dutch oven and add the veal, garlic, onion and dill. Salt and pepper to taste, then cook without browning for 5 minutes. Sprinkle over the flour and nutmeg to coat the veal, then add the chicken stock and water. Bring to a boil, then place in a 375°F oven to bake for 1 hour.

Trim and peel the carrots. Using the white part of the leeks, trim and separate to wash away the always persistent sand. Julienne the carrots and leeks that you have cut into 2 inch lengths.

Heat the 3 ounces of butter in a skillet and cook the vegetables over low heat until wilted.

When the veal comes out of the oven, stir in the vegetable matchsticks, then add cream until the sauce is just as you like. Taste. Dill loses flavor as it cooks so you may want to add more to the blanquette, or sprinkle over the top. Serve with rice. Serves six.

OSSO BUCCO

Some years ago, I stayed for one luxurious night at the Villa d' Este on Lake Como in Italy. A deluxe hotel, it has its own stunning waterfalls and gardens and silk lined elevators. Dining out under the vast striped awning, I was instantly aware of the waiter's indifference. It was the end of the season and the staff was taking off in a day or two to wherever they spent the winter season in Switzerland.

I ordered Osso Bucco, which is a great favorite of mine. The waiter, looking down his nose, announced that this was peasant food, and I should order something else. I refused.

In the end, he won, bringing two of the biggest pieces of veal shank you can imagine. They covered the plate. It was not my finest dining hour.

Anyhow, when you make Osso Bucco, which is perfectly delicious, buy the smallest, meatiest shank you can find. There's a lot of bone, true, but that makes for a lot of flavor.

6 meaty slices of veal shank, 2 inches thick, cut across the marrow bone
salt and fresh ground pepper
flour for dredging
3 tablespoons olive oil
1½ cups chopped onion
½ cup chopped celery
1 cup chopped carrots

2 tablespoons minced garlic
1 teaspoon marjoram
1½ cups dry white wine
2 cups Italian canned tomatoes, chopped somewhat
salt and pepper
1 teaspoon grated lemon rind
2 teaspoons grated orange rind
¼ cup chopped parsley

Salt and pepper the meat, dredge lightly with flour and brown well in the olive oil in your Dutch oven. Take your time browning. Over medium heat it will take 20 minutes at least.

Add the vegetables, garlic and marjoram. Stir in the wine and cook 1 or 2 minutes, then add the tomatoes, salt and pepper to taste. Cover and cook for 1 hour and 15 minutes.

Sprinkle the grated rinds into the stew and cook another 15 minutes, being sure the veal is tender. Serve sprinkled with parsley and accompanied by gnocchi, potato dumplings.

FRANZ PORTMANN'S SWISS VEAL

Franz Portmann is chef at a local club—a totally engaging chap.

Clarified butter: This is important to make when the sautéing is done wholly in butter. Clarified butter does not burn readily. To make it, put the butter in the top of a double boiler to melt over hot water. When the whey settles to the bottom, pour off the clear liquid. That's your clarified butter.

2 pounds veal scallops	1 cup dry white wine
3 ounces clarified butter	½ cup brown gravy
½ cup shallots, finely chopped	1 cup heavy cream
2 cups mushrooms, sliced	salt, white pepper to taste

Cut the veal scallops into matchstick pieces and sauté them lightly in the butter over high heat, tossing about. Do not overcook or they will toughen. Remove from the skillet and keep warm.

Cook the shallots in the same pan, add the mushrooms and sauté lightly. Add the wine and gravy and cook down to half the original quantity. Add the cream and season to taste with salt and pepper. Cook over medium heat until the sauce has the consistency of heavy cream.

Reheat the veal in the sauce but do not boil. Serve with spaetzli or egg noodles. Serves six.

LITTLE VEAL ROASTS WITH MARSALA

4 loin veal chops, 2 inches thick
2 tablespoons flour
½ teaspoon salt
¼ teaspoon fresh ground
   pepper
4 tablespoons butter
½ cup Marsala wine

1½ cups chicken or veal stock
1 onion, chopped
1 carrot, diced
1 stalk celery, chopped
1 tablespoon chopped parsley
½ teaspoon rosemary
½ garlic clove, minced

Dredge the chops in flour mixed with salt and pepper, then brown them in butter in a skillet. Add the wine and let it cook away over medium low heat. The chops will toughen if the heat is too high.

Add half the stock and simmer for 15 minutes, covered. Then transfer the meat to a buttered casserole adding the rest of the stock, the vegetables and seasonings.

Bake about 20 minutes in a 350°F oven. Remove chops and keep warm while you strain the sauce and thicken it if you like. Pour over chops and serve.

VEAL PATTIES WITH MARSALA

Less expensive than veal cutlet, the ground meat is tender and good. Don't for Heaven's sake buy those ready made ones in the butcher's case. Get the veal cubes ground fresh.

2 pounds ground veal
½ cup finely minced onion
1 garlic clove, finely minced
2 teaspoons salt
½ teaspoon white pepper
2 eggs

½ cup flour
½ cup grated Parmesan cheese
¼ cup butter
¼ cup olive oil
1 cup Marsala wine
½ cup chicken broth

Mix the first six ingredients together then shape the mixture into 14 to 16 small patties. Dust lightly with a mixture of flour and Parmesan cheese, and chill for 1 hour.

Heat the butter and oil in a large skillet and brown the patties in it. You'll probably have to do it in two batches. Remove the patties to a warm dish and keep hot while you finish the sauce. Add the Marsala and chicken broth to the skillet, scraping the pan, cooking down until slightly thickened. Taste for seasoning, then serve over the patties. Serves six.

VEAL WITH MUSHROOMS

While this recipe calls for veal scallops, you can use tenders for economy's sake. Just be sure they're thin so that they cook very quickly.

6 veal scallops, pounded thin
1 stick butter (not margarine)
2 large green peppers

1 pound fresh mushrooms
1 cup sherry (dry)
salt and pepper to taste

Seed and slice the green peppers. Quarter the mushrooms. Stir fry in half the butter quickly, tossing lightly as they cook. Add sherry and remove from the heat.

Season the veal with salt and pepper. Sauté in a large skillet in the rest of the butter for about 2 minutes over fairly high heat—they should be lightly browned on each side.

Remove veal to a warm platter and cover with the mushrooms and green peppers. Serves six.

VEAL AND VEGETABLE MOLD (CHOU FARCI)

A fascinating entree from Belgium. The mold is cooked in a water bath and must be covered. The directions say "Cook in a ring mold with a cover in a bain-marie." What we're going to do is cook in a ring mold, securely covered with foil, and set in a pan of water, top of the stove.

2 pounds veal, or veal and pork,
    ground rather coarsely
salt and pepper to taste
1 teaspoon paprika
1 small onion, finely minced
1 garlic clove, finely minced

2 small heads cauliflower,
    cooked al dente, broken into
    flowerets, or an equivalent
    amount of mushrooms or
    broccoli

Combine the meat with the onion and garlic. Season with salt and pepper and paprika.

Butter the mold generously, then layer meat and vegetable, pressing down gently to fill the mold evenly. Set in a pan of water and cook for 1 hour, tightly sealed with foil.

Make a fine bechamel sauce. Turn the mold out on a heated serving platter and serve with bechamel, and new potatoes. Serves eight to ten.

Lamb

BUTTERFLY LEG OF LAMB, GRILLED

In the lexicon of butchery, "butterfly" is almost incongruous in the imagery it provides. Whenever a butcher cuts almost through a piece of meat, then flattens it out to make it both wider and thinner, he butterflies it. A deft butcher will even butterfly that last tiny filet mignon to make an acceptable sized serving. Here it's a leg of lamb, boned, cut almost through, then flattened for broiling.

**1 leg of lamb, (preferably
  small), butterflied**

Marinade:

½ cup Dijon mustard
⅓ cup olive oil
⅓ cup soy sauce
½ cup dry white wine
1 teaspoon crushed or powdered
   rosemary

1 teaspoon powdered ginger
1 garlic clove, minced
juice of 1 lemon

Combine all ingredients in a container which will hold the lamb. Mix well, then marinate the lamb at least twenty four hours.

Grill on your broiler or charcoal grill 15 minutes a side for medium rare.

Allow at least ½ pound lamb per person. Be sure to heat the service plates—of all meats, lamb loves a hot plate most.

BARBECUED LEG OF LAMB

My daughter had this at a friend's house one night and really went on about it. Friend Suzanne Bush parted with the recipe.

6 to 7 pounds leg of lamb, boned, butterflied
1 cup dry red wine
¾ cup beef broth
3 tablespoons orange marmalade
2 tablespoons red wine vinegar

2 tablespoons minced onion
1 tablespoon marjoram
1 tablespoon rosemary
1 big bay leaf, crumbled
1 teaspoon salt
¼ teaspoon ginger
½ teaspoon garlic salt

Combine all ingredients except lamb in a saucepan and simmer, uncovered about 20 minutes.

Trim the lamb of excess fat and place it in a roasting pan. Pour the hot marinade over the lamb and let it stand at room temperature for 6 to 8 hours. Turn it when you think of it, several times.

Barbecue over medium coals for 30 to 45 minutes—the thermometer should read 150°F when it is done. Allow to rest a few minutes, then carve diagonally in thin slices. Serves six to eight.

LAMB FILETS

I beg you, not the lamb patties in the butcher's case. Start with fresh ground lamb and enjoy a different and very rich meat course. You'll only need one to a customer so this will serve eight.

1 medium onion, finely chopped
1 garlic clove, finely minced
1 tablespoon butter
1 tablespoon olive oil
3 or 4 tablespoons milk
1 cup soft white bread crumbs
1¼ pounds lean ground lamb

3 tablespoons chopped parsley
¼ teaspoon rosemary
1 egg
salt, fresh ground pepper
flour for dredging
4 slices lean bacon

In the butter and olive oil, sauté the onions and garlic just until soft. Cool.

In the bottom of a large bowl, soak the bread in the milk then squeeze out the liquid. To the bread, add all remaining ingredients except flour and bacon. Mix well, then shape into 8 patties, dredged in the flour.

Now, cut each slice of bacon in half the long way. You want it long enough to go around the patty, but slim so your lamb is not too, too rich. Take each slice around a patty and tie up with string.

To sauté: When you remove the onion and garlic from the skillet, tilt the pan and leave enough oil for sautéing. Fry the patties over very low heat for about 30 minutes, pouring off fat as it collects.

To broil: Broil rather far away from the heat—you may want to take out the rack and put a pan with a small rack right on the broiler floor. Broil about 12 minutes one side, 5 minutes on the other.

 This was gratefully adapted from a Robert Carrier recipe.

LAMB HASH

A kind of delicious shepherd's pie but with much superior seasoning. This is a fine way to use the leftovers from a leg of lamb.

2 cups leftover cooked lamb
1 medium onion, chopped
1 green pepper, minced
1 tablespoon butter
1 tablespoon chopped parsley
pinch each of rosemary, thyme, marjoram
2 medium tomatoes, seeded, chopped, or, 4 small Italian plum ones, canned, drained

½ cup consommé
½ cup dry white wine
salt and pepper to taste
mashed potatoes for topping
grated Parmesan cheese

Sauté onions and pepper in butter about 5 minutes. Add parsley, herbs, tomatoes, consommé, lamb, wine, salt and pepper. Cover and simmer, very gently, about 1 hour until the flavors come together. Stir occasionally.

Put the lamb mixture in a casserole and top with hot mashed potatoes. Sprinkle with Parmesan and run under the broiler till lovely and brown. Serves four.

IRISH LAMB STEW

One of the world's great dishes, which is hard to find on a restaurant menu except in a really big city, is Irish Lamb Stew. Delicate and very attractive looking, it provides a meal in one with a fine, soothing flavor. Shoulder of lamb is the best cut, but watch your butcher. Traditionally, he cuts it into cubes, bone and all, for stew. Do buy the piece, take the meat off, and cube it, then tie up the bones to add to the pot. Shards of bone are not something I care to serve.

4 pounds lamb shoulder, boned,
    in cubes
water
3 medium onions, chopped
4 potatoes, cut up

3 leeks, chopped
5 stalks celery, chopped
2 garlic cloves, halved
1 tablespoon salt
pinch of cayenne pepper

In a large stew pot or your Dutch oven, cover the lamb and bones with water. Bring to a big boil for about 5 minutes, then discard the water, rinse the meat and pan with cold water, and you're rid of the scum that rises to the surface.

Add 2 quarts of water to the meat, put in all the vegetables and seasonings and bring to a boil again. Simmer over low heat for 1 hour.

Temporarily, remove the meat cubes with a slotted spoon and set aside. Put half the vegetables along with some broth in the blender or processor and purée them. Return to the pan and purée the other half. Add broth to make a fine smooth sauce, not too thick. You're going to cook in it. Hang on to the rest of the original broth in case you need it later.

Now—put the meat back in the pan with the purée and add:

24 tiny white onions (the frozen
    come smaller)
4 potatoes, quartered

6 carrots in sticks about 2 inches
    long

Simmer the lamb with the vegetables another 40 minutes or until the lamb is meltingly tender.

If you like, cook a handful of peas separately at some point. Just before serving, toss them in. They look pretty and add color. Serves six to eight.

BILL'S SHISH KEBAB

When you make this aromatic grilled lamb, Bill suggests buying half a hind leg and cutting the cubes yourself. The butcher does it with such abandon that you end up with chunks laced with tissue, fat, and sometimes even bits of bone. The meat cubes must be tender and excellent in quality. Uniform in size, or the kebabs will not cook properly or be as good as they should.

The Marinade:

½ cup olive oil
1 cup salad oil
2 bay leaves
1 lemon, sliced
1 teaspoon dried thyme
1 teaspoon oregano

½ teaspoon basil
3 garlic cloves
½ teaspoon monosodium
　glutamate
1 teaspoon salt
½ teaspoon black pepper

Combine all ingredients in a large bowl that has a seal-tight lid. Add the lamb cubes and set in the refrigerator for twenty four hours, stirring occasionally.

The Vegetables:

3 green peppers, seeded, cut up
　in large pieces
10 small white onions, peeled

10 cherry tomatoes
10 whole canned mushrooms,
　drained

Alternate marinated meat and vegetables on skewers and cook over a hot charcoal grill, turning and frequently brushing with the marinade.

Serve on a bed of white rice. Bill suggests adding about 8 tablespoons of marinade to the rice while cooking to enhance the flavor and keep the rice moist. Serves eight.

LAMB STEW WITH GREEN BEANS

A wonderful meat stretcher, those green beans. And you can even go farther. Add new potatoes, quartered, or if you have the time, cut them into little balls, and add for the last half hour.

¼ cup olive oil
2 pounds lamb shoulder, cubed
2 pounds green beans
1 medium onion, chopped
¼ cup parsley, minced

2 garlic cloves
1 cup tomato sauce
2 cups water
salt and pepper to taste

Heat the oil in a heavy saucepan and brown the lamb cubes. Add salt, pepper, garlic, onion and parsley.

Trim the beans and cut in half crosswise. Add to the meat. Pour in tomato sauce and water and simmer for 90 minutes until the meat is tender and the sauce somewhat thickened. Serves six.

PARISIAN LAMB STEW

Recently, I encountered a friend I had not seen in the fifteen years since she moved away. After the you-haven't-changed-a-bits and so on, she suddenly peered at me and said, "Do you still make that wonderful lamb stew?" Fifteen years later! I do, and you can if you like.

3 pounds boneless lamb, cubed
⅓ cup vegetable oil
12 small white onions, fresh or frozen
2 tablespoons flour
3 cups meat stock or chicken broth
bouquet garni of parsley, bay leaf and celery, tied together

pinch thyme
1 garlic clove
1 cup tomato puree
salt and pepper
12 small carrot balls
⅓ pound green beans, cut up
½ pound fresh peas
12 potato balls
12 medium mushrooms, sliced
salt and fresh ground pepper

In a large, heavy skillet over high heat, brown the lamb cubes in the vegetable oil, turning and shaking the pan so they do not burn. (This will go faster if you bring the meat to room temperature before you begin.)

Reduce the heat and add the onions, sautéing until they are golden brown. Drain off the oil and put the meat and onions into a Dutch oven. While the skillet is still hot, add a little meat stock to deglaze it and set aside.

Sprinkle lamb and onions with flour, then over heat stir in the meat stock and the liquid from the skillet. Add the bouquet garni, thyme, the whole peeled clove of garlic, and the tomato purée, season with salt and pepper and simmer for about 1 hour, covered.

Using your melon ball cutter, make the carrot and potato balls—they're a little trouble but it does add a touch of class. Add these along with the green beans and peas and cook for another 30 minutes. Somewhere along the way, sauté the mushroom slices briefly in butter and add in the last 10 minutes of cooking.

Taste for seasoning—the vegetables will take up a lot of the salt. Season again, remove the bouquet garni and serve in heated rimmed soup plates, garnished with chopped parsley.

 Be ready for, "Is there any more?" People do want seconds of this surprisingly good stew. It should feed six, but four will eat it up. With it, a big green salad, good bread and red wine.

The Fire Maker

When the sweet warm air of summer arrives, and the sound of the lawn mower is heard in the land, a visible phenomenon occurs in American suburbs.

At dinnertime, countless thin wisps of smoke rise up from countless back yards, terraces, patios, and decks. Behind the Victorian mansion, the glassy contemporary, the 1929 bungalow, America is barbecuing.

Generally speaking, this is man's work. Cooking over coals seems to bring out some primal instinct in him, and even men who wouldn't lift a finger in the kitchen will cook with a will out of doors. With some suggestion of the aboriginal, he arranges and rearranges the coals, spears the meat, and at all times wears a rather lordly air. He makes appreciative sounds when you, his mate, come out of the cave from time to time bearing gifts, like a Scotch on the rocks, or a martini.

Before the fire, he selects the steak, or deplores the amount of fat in, or not in, the ground beef. Have you watched him prepare a marinade? Gravely, he measures, stirs, and tastes. This is serious business.

You can turn this atavism into a sterling benefit—here's your chance for a free afternoon and a night out, outside at any rate. By preparing his props in the morning, making the supporting dishes ahead, you can clear out for the afternoon. Come dinnertime, you can sit back like a lady, sip your aperitif, and the only price of admission is that you make admiring noises occasionally.

(Naturally, being a smart lady, you have trained the children in KP and the paper chase.)

Make aheads to go along with grilled meats or fish are legion. Baked stuffed potatoes to be briefly re-heated. Casseroles of potatoes or beans. Fine flavored rice if he's got an Oriental urge. Good old reliable baked beans when the budget says hot dogs. Big salads. A fry pan full of sliced onions cooked forever, limp and delicious, will get rounds of applause, again reheated.

(Once my son said to me of those onions, "Mother, you could bottle these and sell them.")

If your tastes go more to green than dried beans, make little foil packets in the morning. Arrange three or four fresh vegetables to a serving, season, add butter, then seal up the package. Lay them on the grill 15 or 20 minutes before the meal is supposed to begin. A nice combo is eggplant, tomato, onion and a mushroom or two, but you can do single vegetables the same way.

The barbecue opens up another dizzy vista. If your man, like so many men, is difficult to buy presents for, now you have it made. Countless accessories and embellishments for the practies of his art will delight him. Gloves, long handled tools, various fire starters, bigger and better grills, a double-hinged grill for thin fillets of fish or other breakables, a meat thermometer if he's into rotisserie, they'll get you stars in your crown.

Encouraged and admired, the outdoor cook may even get so interested that he wants to make this a year-round hobby.

Then maybe at Christmas, you'll get that range you've wanted greedily and passionately for several years. You know the one that does absolutely everything, up to, and including, charcoal grilling? Whee!

Fowl Play...

Consider the Chicken

In the late twenties, the politicians promised us a chicken in every pot. Now we've got it, yea verily, we're stuck with it since chicken is about what we can afford in these times.

But facing a certain menu monotony is not at all bad when it involves this excellent bird who now comes plumper, juicier and more versatile than ever before.

In the language, chicken has a time honored connotation. Because this fowl is a nervous wreck, tends to flee wildly squawking when approached, the word has come to mean faint hearted. Chicken!

Even when used a very different way, it got turned around and is used negatively. For instance, we never say about a pretty young woman, "She's some chicken," but we sometimes say about an older woman, "She's no Spring chicken."

Chicken crops up in every cuisine and is universally cooked, which means there are an almost infinite number of fine ways to deal with it, whether it's a tender young thing or a large mature bird. Our beautiful plump crossbred chickens are a far cry from earlier stringy versions, but you should still exercise judgment when buying.

The very young chicken has a flexible breast bone. Feel it. The two to four pound baby is perhaps two months old and being tender, is best broiled, fried or roasted. Stewing will do him in—you want a bigger bird for that.

For roasting, the ideal size is four to seven pounds. Even better for this purpose is the capon—the eunuch of the flock. At the height of Rome's profligate trip down the primrose path, it was worrisome to the town fathers that too many egg laying hens were being served at too many banquets.

They passed a law forbidding the slaughter of hens. As a supreme piece of serendipity, when the poultry men performed a simple surgical operation, they created the capon, bigger, plumper and better with a flavorful layer of fat just under the skin. Hard on the rooster, but great for us.

If you do buy a frozen bird, look at it closely. If there is pinkish ice under the wrap, it has probably been frozen, thawed, and refrozen. Avoid.

Cutting up and boning the chicken yourself will save you money, and with a sharp boning knife and good kitchen scissors, it really isn't too difficult. Practice first on Chinese dishes where you're going to cut up the boned chicken anyhow. You'll soon be able to produce a handsome boned breast at considerable savings.

Not the least of the fowl's virtues is the giving up of fine flavorful stock. When you cook chicken for salad, the cooking broth, well seasoned can be the basis for many soups, give a great taste to vegetables and certainly add flavor to rice.

Not too many people have clay pots, but if you do, you can achieve the ultimate in roasted chicken. It comes out browned and glowing, so moist inside that the juices almost leap out when you cut.

You probably do have lemons, and one of the classiest ways to cook an Italian style chicken is to stuff it, not with bread stuffing, but with one or two well pierced lemons, salt and pepper outside, and that's it. Roast 15 minutes breast side down, at 350°F, turn and roast another 20 minutes, then turn the heat up to 400°F for browning. The skin will be crisp and brown, and may balloon. The meat, flavored with the lemons is superb. One caution: if the lemon has a very heavy rind, make the holes large. I have had them close up.

Chicken happily combines with all sorts of herbs and spices. It takes up marinade well and barbecues beautifully. You can stew it, roast it, fry it, sauté it, eat it cold or hot, make soup or salad with it and go international at the same time.

Some chicken! Some bird!

GEORGETTE'S CHICKEN AND HAM CASSEROLE

The first time I read through the ingredients, I could hardly wait to try it for a buffet. It serves eight.

1 cup flour
2 teaspoons salt
1 teaspoon pepper
1 teaspoon summer savory
4 whole chicken breasts, boned, halved
¼ cup butter or margarine
4 thin slices cooked ham
1 pound fresh mushrooms
2 medium onions, chopped

1 garlic clove, crushed
1 tablespoon minced parsley
½ cup chicken broth
½ cup dry sherry
½ cup orange juice
2 teaspoons brown sugar
2 heads Belgian endive, quartered
1 package frozen peas (10-ounce size)

In a paper bag, combine the flour, salt, pepper and savory. Shake the chicken pieces in the mixture, a few at a time. They should be just lightly floured.

Brown the chicken in a heavy skillet in butter or oil, and when golden, remove and drain on paper towels. Cut the ham slices in half, roll up and secure with toothpicks then brown in the same skillet. Drain and set aside.

To the skillet add any remaining butter. In it, sauté the mushrooms, onions, and garlic seasoned with the parsley, salt and pepper. When the vegetables are tender, add chicken broth, sherry, brown sugar and orange juice. Cook, stirring easily, about 5 minutes.

In a large shallow baking dish, arrange the chicken breasts alternately with the ham rolls (don't forget to remove the toothpicks). Pour the sauce from the skillet over all, then cover with a lid or foil. Bake at 350°F for 1 hour.

Remove the cover and rebaste. Place the endive quarters and chunks of frozen peas between the chicken and ham rolls. Recover and bake 15 minutes more, basting halfway. Serve with rice. Serves eight.

ALGERIAN CHICKEN

8 chicken thighs, or,
8 half breasts or,
4 of each
paprika
2 tablespoons butter
½ cup chicken broth
1 can tomatoes in juice, medium
    size, or, 3 whole tomatoes,
    chopped with juice

1 garlic clove, crushed
2 small eggplants, peeled and
    cubed
1 medium onion, chopped
½ teaspoon each thyme,
    rosemary, black pepper
1 tablespoon minced parsley

Sprinkle chicken pieces with paprika. In a large skillet, melt the butter and brown the chicken on both sides. Remove from the pan and set aside for the moment.

Deglaze the pan with the broth, scraping up the brown bits, then add the vegetables and garlic and sprinkle with all the seasonings.

Return the chicken to the skillet and simmer, covered, about 30 minutes. (If you prefer, you can bake in a covered casserole for 45 minutes at 350°F.)

Serve with kasha, couscous, rice or noodles. Serves four.

CHICKEN BREASTS WITH SHALLOT BUTTER

The Hotel DuPont serves a marvelous breast of capon in its banquet department. I was able to get the recipe for the filling, but we can't do it the way they do it. The hotel has a machine which forces the stuffing into the breast so that it does not have to be cut.

After some experimenting, I found two fine ways to make this, using chicken breasts rolled. This is for six.

12 half chicken breasts,
    skinned, boned, medium size
1 cup butter
1 cup margarine
1 cup fine dry white bread
    crumbs

1 cup finely minced shallots
4 tablespoons dry white wine
salt and pepper

Method I: Flatten the breasts, but be careful not to tear. Let the butter and margarine become soft, then mix with all ingredients. Lightly salt and pepper the flattened breasts, then divide the filling among them, spreading it on the larger half of the breast.

Roll up firmly then dip in:

2 whole eggs, beaten, then in
fine dry bread crumbs

Be sure the ends of the rolls are egg and crumb covered, too. Now, chill the rolls so that the butter filling becomes very firm.

Method II: Let the butter and margarine become soft and mix with all ingredients. Put the mixture in the refrigerator until very cold and hard.

Divide the mixture and make 12 hard sticks of it, like throwaway cigarette lighters but maybe fatter. Lightly salt the breasts then wrap them around the solid stuffing. Dip in the egg and crumbs and chill again.

To finish the dish:

Put about ¼ cup of clarified butter in a heavy skillet that will hold the rolls. Over medium heat, brown lightly to make a sealer and keep the butter-filling in. Reduce heat and finish cooking, turning several times. It will take about 12 minutes, but longer won't hurt. Just don't let them get too brown.

It works either way, and you finally have a tender, delicious roll with a flavorful middle.

If you like, make a very light mushroom sauce for this, using the butter in the skillet to sauté the mushrooms. Sprinkle flour over then, add chicken stock and cream to finish.

But you don't really need the sauce.

CHICKEN BREASTS IN SHERRY

¼ cup fine dry bread crumbs
1 teaspoon salt
dash garlic salt
pinch of tarragon
2 tablespoons grated Parmesan
   cheese
4 half chicken breasts, boned,
   skinned

4 slices Virginia ham
4 thin slices Swiss cheese
flour for dredging
1 egg beaten
2 tablespoons butter
½ cup dry sherry
½ cup chicken broth

Combine crumbs, salt, garlic salt, tarragon and grated cheese in a shallow bowl. Set aside.

Flatten the breasts thin. Place a slice of ham, a slice of cheese on each and roll up. Dip the rolls into flour, shaking off excess, then into beaten egg, then coat with the crumb mixture.

Brown the rolls in melted butter in a skillet. Arrange in a baking dish where they fit nicely, then add the sherry and broth. Bake for 30 minutes at 350°F. Serves four.

STUFFED CHICKEN BREASTS EPICURE

Fancy, but delicious for a small perfect dinner. You can make ahead to the baking point, and spend a minimum of time in the kitchen just before dinner.

¼ cup raisins, marinated in 1
   ounce cognac, 1 ounce white
   wine
½ cup blanched almonds
   ground
½ apple, peeled, cored and
   diced
1 tablespoon butter
1 small onion, minced fine
3 chicken livers, chopped fine
4 large mushrooms, chopped
   fine

1 tablespoon parsley, chopped
1 tablespoon chives, chopped
1 egg
3 tablespoons cream
4 whole chicken breasts, boned
   and halved
salt and pepper
1 stick butter, melted
sauce Supreme

Marinate the raisins and set aside. Buzz the almonds in the blender or grind, and sauté lightly in butter. Set aside. Dice the apple.

In a small skillet, sauté the onion until it is transparent, add chicken livers and mushrooms, parsley, chives, and cook for a few minutes over fairly high heat. Take off heat.

Whisk the egg with the cream and stir into the liver mixture. Add the almonds and diced apple. Strain the raisins and add, reserving the marinade. Season this stuffing mixture to taste, then chill.

(All of this can be done early in the day. You can continue with the recipe and stuff the breasts as well, keeping them refrigerated until dinner time.)

Flatten each half chicken breast, and divide the stuffing among them. Roll the chicken firmly around the filling, and arrange, seam side down in a baking dish where they fit nicely.

Season lightly and baste with melted butter. Bake at 450°F for just 5 minutes, then reduce heat to 325°F and bake 25 minutes longer, basting once or twice.

Sauce Supreme: Make a bechamel sauce using light cream instead of milk, plus the reserved marinade to flavor. One and a half cups of sauce will be enough.

To serve: Place 2 chicken rolls on each plate and spoon the sauce over. Serves four.

CHICKEN BREASTS FLAMBÉ

6 chicken breasts, halved,
   skinned and boned
salt, white pepper
½ cup butter or margarine
3 tablespoons chopped green
   onions

4 tablespoons Amaretto liqueur
4 tablespoons brandy
2 egg yolks
1 cup light cream
1 tablespoon dried tarragon

Season the chicken with salt and pepper and sauté in half the butter in a large skillet. Remove to a platter and keep warm.

In the remaining butter, cook the onions until wilted, add 2 tablespoons of the Amaretto and deglaze the pan, scraping the bottom. Beat the egg yolks with the cream and gradually add them to the pan juices in the skillet, cooking, stirring until the sauce is thickened—better if it doesn't boil. Remove from the heat and add the tarragon.

Combine the remaining liqueur with the brandy, warm it, and blaze the chicken pieces. When the fire goes out, pour the sauce over the chicken and serve.

How many will this serve? If you have very large pieces of chicken and many other things on the menu, one apiece would serve twelve. If you buy smaller breasts, you'll need two to a customer.

CHICKEN IN WINE

Coq au vin my way. I really don't like wet chicken, and every time I've eaten it in France, it has come skin on, in a very thin liquid, and on the whole unattractive. This is the way I make it at home.

3 whole chicken breasts, halved
6 large chicken thighs
2 slices lean salt pork
flour for dredging
1 stick butter or margarine
12 small white onions
½ pound mushrooms, sliced

1 garlic clove, minced
1 bay leaf
sprig of parsley
salt and pepper
¼ cup cognac
2 cups dry red wine

Dice the salt pork and render it in a Dutch oven until the pieces are crisp and browned. Remove and drain, then set aside.

Dredge the chicken pieces with flour (easiest in a paper bag). Shake off any excess flour and brown the chicken thoroughly in the drippings plus the butter. You may need to do half at a time, setting half aside.

Put all the chicken back in the pan, warm the cognac, pour it over the chicken and blaze. When the fire is out, add the wine.

Put in the onions, mushrooms, bay leaf, parsley, garlic and the lardons—the little salt pork dice. Put in a 300°F oven and braise for about 2½ hours.

When the chicken is really tender, I depart from tradition and remove it from the pot. Take the vegetables out with a slotted spoon and arrange them in the bottom of a baking dish. Lay the chicken pieces over and pour all that sauce over everything.

Put in a 350°F oven for 30 minutes or so, basting the chicken several times. The sauce is reduced and more flavorful. Just don't let the sauce disappear. Serve with wild and white rice to six.

CHICKEN CHEESE CASSEROLE

Assemble this easy casserole ahead and pop in the oven a half hour before dinner. If you have leftover chicken, fine. Whether you do, or cook some chicken to make this, try to have a mix of white and dark meat for better flavor.

2 cups cooked chicken, cubed
1 cup diced celery
¼ cup sliced stuffed green
  olives
1 tablespoon grated onion
1 tablespoon lemon juice
4 good twists of fresh ground
  pepper

1 teaspoon salt
½ cup mayonnaise
¼ pound real Cheddar cheese,
  grated
Optional: ¼ cup slivered
  almonds

Combine all ingredients except the cheese in a bowl. Season to taste then turn into a casserole and sprinkle the top with cheese. Bake about 25 minutes at 375°F, or until the cheese bubbles. Serves four. Double for eight.

BRANDIED CHICKEN LIVERS

For a brunch or supper, this is a dandy dish served over toasted English muffins, or if you prefer, rice.

4 tablespoons butter
¼ pound fresh mushrooms
  sliced
4 green onions, chopped
1 pound chicken livers, patted
  dry
¼ cup brandy

flour
¾ cup half and half or milk
¾ cup chicken broth
salt and pepper
English muffins or cooked
  rice

In 2 tablespoons of the butter, sauté mushrooms and onions until onions are soft. Remove from the skillet with a slotted spoon, then add to the skillet the chicken livers, cut in half or bite size pieces. Season with salt and pepper.

Warm the brandy, pour over the livers and blaze. When the fire is out, return the mushrooms and onions to the skillet and toss, after sprinkling with about 2 tablespoons of flour.

Add the milk and chicken stock and simmer gently until the sauce thickens. Season again, then serve over buttered, toasted muffins or rice. Serves four.

PECAN CHICKEN

Simple and superb, this chicken can be served hot or at room temperature. This has been one of the favorite reader recipes. From Virginia Hanby.

2 cut up chickens (3 pounders) or, an equivalent amount of breasts
½ pound coarsely chopped pecans

1 cup sour cream
1 cup light cream
salt and pepper
1½ sticks butter, melted

Mix sour and light cream together. Dip chicken pieces in the cream, then in pecans. Arrange the pieces on a shallow baking dish (a jelly roll pan works fine) that has been spread liberally with melted butter.

Place in a 350°F oven and bake for 1 hour and 15 minutes, basting at least twice with the rest of the melted butter.

To make a sauce when the chicken is done, put the pan juices in a saucepan, bring just to a boil and add enough cream to thicken.

CHICKEN POT PIE

A famous regional dish called a pie, but actually chicken with the famous slippery dumplings so admired in the mid-Atlantic area.

1 stewing chicken, whole or cut up	2 stalks celery
2 or 3 onions	3 quarts water (more if needed)
	salt and pepper to taste

Cook the chicken, onions and celery in water until tender. Taste for seasoning. Remove chicken and keep warm.

Slippery Dumplings

3 cups flour	ice water, enough to make a dough
1½ teaspoons salt	
3 tablespoons shortening or lard	

Put flour, salt and shortening in a bowl. Cut in the shortening and enough ice water to make a dough. Knead on a floured board, then roll out in a thin sheet. Cut into 2 inch squares.

As soon as the chicken is removed from the broth, raise the heat so it boils, then toss in the squares and cook for 10 minutes with the lid on.

Return the chicken to the pot, reheat and serve. Serves four to six depending on the size of the chicken.

CHICKEN AND WILD RICE CASSEROLE

This is a family favorite that will do beautifully for eight at a party. But if you have four at home, make two smaller casseroles and freeze one.

3 pounds chicken breasts and thighs
1 cup water
1 cup dry sherry
1½ teaspoons salt
½ teaspoon curry powder
1 medium onion, quartered

1 stalk celery with leaves
1 package wild and white rice (12 ounce)
1 pound fresh mushrooms
1 cup sour cream
1 can cream of mushroom soup (10¾ ounces)

Put the chicken into a large kettle and add the water, sherry, salt, curry powder, onion and celery. Simmer until tender.

Remove from the heat, strain the broth and reserve it to cook the rice in. Cool the chicken and remove skin and bones, then dice into fairly large cubes.

Cook the wild and white rice, substituting the chicken broth for water, and using all (or part) of the seasonings that come with the rice. All seems a bit much considering the many good ingredients in this dish.

Melt some butter in a skillet and sauté the sliced mushrooms briefly. Add to the chicken along with the cooked rice, then turn into a greased 3 to 3½-quart casserole.

Combine the sour cream with the mushroom soup and spread over the top. Bake, uncovered, in a 350°F oven for about 30 minutes. If you have to hold it a while longer, reduce the heat and cover with foil.

HOT CHICKEN SALAD

This will serve twelve for a buffet, and it couldn't be easier to assemble. If you make it ahead, be sure the casserole is at room temperature when it goes into the oven.

9 cups cooked chicken, cubed
3 cups celery, chopped fine
1½ cups slivered almonds,
    browned in butter

2 cups mayonnaise
1½ teaspoons salt
6 teaspoons grated onion
6 tablespoons lemon juice

Combine all ingredients. Turn into a buttered baking dish, not a deep one, an oval or oblong au gratin is best. Bake at 450°F for 10 minutes.

While the casserole bakes, make the topping:

1½ cups grated sharp Cheddar
    cheese

2½ cups broken up potato chips
½ cups chopped almonds

Combine and distribute evenly over the chicken. Reduce heat to 350°F and bake another 20 minutes.

SWEET POTATO SAUSAGE STUFFING

If your family is too small for a giant turkey on those special occasions, consider the many virtues of the capon, a fine meaty fowl of excellent flavor. The following dressing will do for a six to seven pound bird—for a change.

. can sweet potatoes (1 pound,
    7 ounces)
6 big fresh mushrooms, chopped
1 small garlic clove, minced

1 medium onion, chopped
½ pound bulk sausage
salt and fresh ground pepper
powdered sage to taste

Mash the drained sweet potatoes smooth in a bowl. In a skillet, sauté the mushrooms, garlic and onion in butter until tender, about 5 minutes. Add to the sweet potatoes.

Without washing the skillet, add the sausage, breaking it up as you sauté it, until the fat is rendered. Drain the sausage thoroughly and combine it with the sweet potato mixture. Season with salt and pepper then carefully add the sage, starting with just a little, adding more as it pleases you.

CHICKEN WITH WALNUTS

Cook and teacher Pat Tabibian says this is her own family's favorite chicken recipe. She acquired it when studying at the Culinary Institute of America.

3 whole chicken breasts
   skinned and boned
1 teaspoon sugar
1 teaspoon salt
1 tablespoon soy sauce
3 tablespoons dry sherry
¾ cup water
2 tablespoons cornstarch

1 egg, lightly beaten
¼ cup peanut oil
1 cup walnuts, broken up
½ teaspoon ground ginger
2 garlic cloves, minced
1 can bamboo shoots, drained,
   slivered (5 ounces)

Cut the meat of the chicken breasts into bite size pieces. In a bowl, make a marinade of the sugar, salt, soy sauce and sherry. Marinate the chicken in this for at least 20 minutes, at room temperature. When you remove the chicken, add ¾ cup of water to the marinade and set aside.

Sprinkle the chicken evenly with the cornstarch, then dip into the beaten egg. Heat the oil in a wok or a deep skillet, brown the walnuts in the oil and remove with a slotted spoon. Set aside.

Sauté the chicken, ginger and garlic until lovely and golden brown, tossing as you go. Add the water-marinade mixture, cover and simmer for 15 minutes. Remove the lid, add the bamboo shoots and the browned walnuts, then simmer uncovered for 5 more minutes. Serve with rice to five or six.

SWEET AND SOUR CHICKEN

Nice and easy dinner for six, full of flavor. Serve with plain rice.

3 pounds cut up chicken
½ cup butter or margarine

Mix some dredging flour with:

¼ teaspoon salt　　　　　　　**¼ teaspoon garlic salt**
¼ teaspoon celery salt　　　　**¼ teaspoon nutmeg**

Shake the chicken in a paper bag so that the flour mixture coats it lightly all over. Shake off excess flour.

Heat the butter in a skillet and brown the chicken over moderate heat. Arrange the chicken pieces in a baking dish and strew over them:

1 can pineapple tidbits, drained
**　　(12 ounces)**

Reserve the pineapple juice for the sauce.

Sauce:

1 cup pineapple juice　　　　**1 tablespoon sugar**
3 tablespoons flour　　　　　**⅓ cup soy sauce**

Put the chicken skillet back on the heat and sprinkle the flour over the drippings. Add the sugar and soy sauce then the pineapple juice. Scrape the bottom to get the brown bits and cook, stirring until you have a sauce, thickened and smooth. Pour this over the chicken pieces and bake at 350°F for 1 hour.

Sometimes I put some nice squares of green pepper in this, partly for flavor, partly for appearance.

TURKEY HASH STRETCHED (OR CHICKEN)

A reader sent this to me and it seems good to me on several counts: First, it tastes good, second, it uses 3 cups of leftover turkey and third, it stretches that leftover to serve six. All that in half an hour.

1 can chicken broth
¾ cup water
1 teaspoon salt
dash pepper
1 package dry hashed brown
    potatoes (5½ ounces)
½ cup finely chopped onion

½ cup finely chopped green
    pepper
½ cup margarine
3 cups chopped cooked turkey or
    chicken
¼ cup sour cream

Combine chicken broth, water, salt and pepper in a saucepan. Bring to a boil, add the potatoes and let them reconstitute for 10 minutes off the heat.

Sauté onions and green peppers in some of the margarine. In a bowl, combine the turkey, the potato mixture, the ¼ cup sour cream and mix together. Add this to the skillet, stirring in the onions and peppers. Add more margarine, if needed, then sauté until the bottom is crusty and brown. Turn, as you can, and brown the other side.

Sauce:

1 can cream of mushroom soup
    (10¾ ounces)

¼ cup sour cream

Heat together and serve with the browned hash.

Food and the Big Laugh

An entertaining way to consider food is in the context of characters in literature, or the theater, or TV.

Can you ever again look at a plate of oysters on the half shell without summoning up Tom Jones and his lady—well, whatever she was—in one of the funniest, sexiest scenes ever to hit film?

Take a bowl of gruel. In the mind's eye is Oliver. More, please. The epitome of the underprivileged.

Spinach. Even if you're Urdu or Lapp or Thai, you immediately see that scrawny arm, that tennis-ball muscle, that Popeye who did more for spinach than Birdseye did for freezers.

Cucumber sandwiches. Delicately funny, they provide some of the best props that ever hit a stage when Oscar Wilde points out the importance of being Ernest.

Here are five words: "But it's the best butter," and there you are, down the rabbit hole with Alice and friends.

Lollipop—take your pick. Shirley or Kojack.

Show anyone a custard pie, and he will instantly recall reel after reel of slapstick peopled with Charlie Chase and Harry Langdon and Harold Lloyd and Buster Keaton in silent, horrendous, open-mouthed outrage.

Show anyone a pan of beans and a fire and he'll put the cowpoke in. Show him a charred steak, big as a platter, and he'll know the Duke's in town and action is imminent.

Grapes. Very interesting. In old films, sirens and hedonistic monarchs were always portrayed eating grapes the hard way, from a hanging position about a foot above the head, one at a time, while the actors looked sultry. This was supposed to indicate the dissolution of the faded femme fatale or the jaded emperor. Chavez would have had a fit.

Mae West handled it with more brevity and gave us a classic one-liner. Remember? "Peel me a grape, Beulah."

Food and drink has always been a quickie way to establish character, simplistically. The actor orders wine and goes on and on about vintage, temperature, shape of glass and attributes. We know he's sophisticated.

Let him order Maneschewitz—he's a klutz.

As a comic device, food has proven useful. Consider the rubber chicken flung about the stage with abandon. What makes a naked chicken funny? Bare, forlorn, limp and pale, it still elicits howls from the vaudeville audience.

How about the banana skin. See the solid citizen toss a banana peel over his shoulder as Ben Blue comes into view. Everyone automatically writes the rest of that scenario.

The holes in Swiss cheese are funny. Jello is funny. Cakes that rise, then collapse are funny. Remember that famous Laurel and Hardy short that devolved on a gigantic cake that fell to the flat tire stage? The boys inflated it with bicycle pump. Then it was up, down, up, down until the whole thing exploded along with the audience.

If the small town politician got too bombastic, it was a tomato that cut him down to size. And in film after film, the egg broke. It broke in the comic's hat, streaming down his face; in his pocket, from which emerged that viscous hand; on his chair, a situation which gave rise to some prolonged double takes.

Soup is funny—the noises made while consuming, flies in same, eddies and mysterious currents within the plate.

Spaghetti is a scream with the long build up of getting it around the fork, the tortuous trip to the mouth, the inhalation, protracted and messy: and finally, to go the whole way, the plate updumped on the head, like some wayward hat with a thousand streamers.

*   *   *

There is probably not one of you reading this who has not had some absolutely dreadful thing happen in your kitchen—so awful—such a mess that in the end you stood laughing uncontrollably at food unleashed. Soup on the ceiling? A blown-up potato in the oven? You know. It's so bad, it's funny.

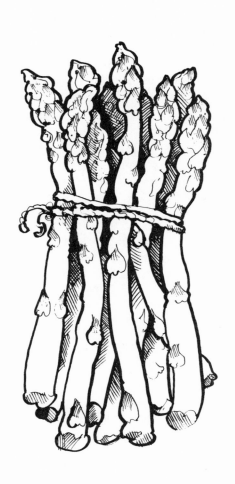

From the Ground Up...

Various Vegetables

You may have noticed more vegetable recipes in this book than the number for any other foods. There's a reason.

The vegetable has always been the overlooked part of our cuisine. In a restaurant, the waitress will say, "The vegetable today is . . ." while the huge menu has a mind boggling list of entrees.

You've heard yourself at home. . .Serving steak for dinner, you frequently think, "I guess I'll get some frozen peas out of the freezer." It's often a last minute thought.

With the spiraling cost of meats, vegetables will now play a very much more important part of your menu, if you'll let them. And your family will enjoy them, if you'll cook them with some flair.

Many vegetables are the better for being cooked in a little chicken broth. Some, like carrots, want a pinch of sugar. Peas are enhanced cooked in the outside leaf of a head of lettuce. Celery, white onions and leeks want a cream sauce. The celery will take a bit of white wine; the white onions a bit of sherry; the leeks prefer to be au gratined.

Lots of people don't care for cabbage, broccoli and Brussels sprouts but it's probably because they haven't had them cooked very interestingly. Tiny sprouts can be partially cooked in salted water, then drained and finished in butter in a skillet, sprinkled with rosemary.

Most cabbage is served overcooked and flavorless. Served pale green, slightly al dente with a bit of caraway seed, and butter it's a delight.

You buy mixed vegetables in the supermarket. Why not make them at home? Don't cook them together, but cook a package, or a fresh pound of each, separately. Then put them together with pimento, green pepper, parsley, onion, seasonings of all sorts, and freeze them in servings for four or six.

So many recipes call for tomatoes that when they come in like a flood, midsummer, you should gather up all you can. Cook into sauce, pureé them and freeze. One suggestion about using canned or stewed tomatoes in a dish: cook them down for 30 minutes or so before measuring for the recipe. Much, much better.

There are certain vegetables that I feel are good meat substitutes, eggplant for one. You somehow get the feeling that you've eaten meat after a substantial dish containing eggplant. Sweet potatoes are another. A half of a big baked sweet potato, rich with butter adds a good sturdy touch to a green vegetable plate.

Two vegetables I really prefer just as they are—peas and asparagus. Fresh peas with butter, asparagus the same, are exquisite tastes.

Zucchini is now the In vegetable and rightly so, since it is so versatile. Raw in salads, barely cooked in butter as a side dish, the basis of ratatouille and many other mixtures, it even goes into breads.

Just to remind you that there are more adventurous vegetables to try, test your group out with artichokes some night. One to a person, boiled in salted water with a bit of lemon juice, they're done when a leaf pulls out easily. Dip in melted butter or Hollandaise hot, or in French dressing or mayonnaise if cold.

Cucumbers can be cooked. A very good way is to cut in half longwise, seed and make a hollow. Parboil about 5 minutes, then fill with a stuffing of your choice, as you would stuff zucchini. Top with crumbs and bake about 20 minutes at 375°F.

If you get turned-up noses when turnips are mentioned, try this: peel and cube young white or yellow turnips, and cook until tender in salted water. Drain, then add some butter and sprinkle with sugar. Keep on cooking, sprinkling with more sugar until they are glazed. They are excellent with pork or veal.

There is a prevalence of potatoes just ahead. One reason is that statistically, in a year, an American will eat one hundred and thirteen pounds of potatoes as opposed to ninety-five pounds of fresh vegetables, fifty-two pounds of canned, and nine pounds of frozen.

The other reason is that I'm crazy about potatoes.

ASPARAGUS PIE

When the asparagus is in full supply, fresh, and you feel like having company, try this quiche like dish which tastes as good at room temperature as it does hot.

3 pounds fresh asparagus
salt, pepper and nutmeg to taste
4 tablespoons butter
¾ cup grated Gruyère or Swiss
   cheese

1 cup shredded prosciutto ham
4 eggs, well beaten
4 tablespoons or more Romano
   cheese

Cook asparagus as usual until tender. Drain, then cut the stalks into bite size pieces, removing any tough ends. Return the asparagus to the saucepan, season and add the butter.

As soon as the butter melts, toss lightly then turn into a buttered 9 or 10 inch pie plate. Make the asparagus layer even, then sprinkle with the grated cheese, the prosciutto and pour the beaten eggs over all. Top with the Romano and bake in a 350°F oven for 30 to 40 minutes. The eggs will be set and the top will have a golden crust. Serves six to eight.

THE BEST GREEN BEANS

Restaurant green beans are an abomination. There is no reason why they could not be done this way—deliciously.

For six people, buy 2 pounds of the firmest, freshest green beans you can lay hands on. Trim, wash, then put in some ice water to crisp while you bring to a rapid boil the biggest pot of water you can handle. Add salt, and when the boiling is fast and furious, drop in the beans, a few at a time, so as not to stop the boiling.

Cook till al dente—crisp and firm. It will take about 10 minutes, but try one to make sure. Drain quickly and rinse with cold water to stop the cooking and refresh the beans. Dry the beans on paper towels and keep them in the refrigerator until serving time.

Then you can go wherever you like. Simply reheated in a pan with melted butter, seasoned with salt and pepper, they are fine. But if you fancy it, add some dill. Or top them with buttered crumbs. Whatever.

You can cook these in the morning, and serve them for dinner without any loss of flavor or texture.

BROCCOLI PIEMONTESE

You can use frozen stalks for this, but the fresh is so much better. Of all the frozen vegetables, it seems to me that broccoli goes limpest, fastest. It should be almost crisp done in this style.

1 bunch fresh broccoli	**salt and pepper**
2 garlic cloves	**½ cup dry white wine**
olive oil	

Discarding the heavy stems, take the flowerets off the broccoli. Put some olive oil in a heavy skillet and sauté the garlic gently. Add the flowerets and cook gently, spooning all over and seasoning with salt and pepper. When tender-crisp, turn up the heat, put in the white wine and cook a few minutes longer. Serves four to six.

CARROTS COGNAC

If you have a processor, this recipe is child's play. The carrot is so underrated by many people that it's always a pleasure to prove its great taste. All it needs is a little help—in this case, cognac.

2 bunches carrots, trimmed, scraped	**1 teaspoon sugar**
½ cup butter	**salt**
	¼ cup cognac

Slice the carrots very thin in the processor. If you do them by hand, it goes faster if you take a thin slice off one side of each carrot to keep it from rolling while you slice. I use a thin cleaver to do this by hand.

Melt the butter in a baking dish that has a close fitting cover. Stir in sugar and salt. Put in the carrots and cognac and bake in a 350°F oven for 45 to 50 minutes until tender, not brown.

 Once I interviewed Julia Child for my paper, and in the course of conversation, she remarked on how you now see women holding up bunches of carrots, or inspecting cucumbers or whatever in the market, not inspecting for flaws, but visually measuring for the processor. Will they fit?

CREAMED CELERY

This is from sister Irene who thinks everyone ought to get in the habit of cooking celery for itself.

2 cups celery stalks, sliced across	1 tablespoon minced onion
salt and pepper	2 tablespoons flour
2 tablespoons butter	½ cup cream
	¼ cup chicken broth

In a small heavy saucepan with a tight fitting lid, put the celery, butter and salt and pepper to cook slowly over very low heat until the celery is almost tender, about 16 minutes. Add the onion and cook until that is tender. When all is right, there should be practically no liquid remaining in the pan.

Blend in the flour and gradually add the chicken broth and cream. Cook until the sauce thickens. This will serve four.

 At the end, take a bit on a teaspoon and put just a touch of nutmeg on to see if you like it. I do, although it isn't in the original recipe.

SOUTHERN CORN PUDDING

When you're serving a meal that needs some holding down, some sturdy addition, corn pudding comes into its own.

butter	1 teaspoon baking powder
2 eggs, well beaten	1 cup light cream (or milk)
1½ tablespoons flour	2 cups fresh corn cut off the cob
2 tablespoons sugar	or, 1 medium can cream-
1 teaspoon salt	style corn

Melt a piece of butter the size of an egg in a casserole. (Already you can see that it's southern!)

Combine all ingredients except corn in a bowl and mix well. Add corn. Turn the mixture into the casserole and bake for 30 to 45 minutes in a 350°F oven. Serves four.

 The time variance is due to the corn. If you use canned it will take longer than if you use fresh because of the extra liquid. You bake until set.

EGGPLANT CAPONATA

A versatile dish to be served as is, or used as a crepe filling. Grated Monterey Jack cheese provides a good topping for the crepes.

1 medium to large eggplant	1 small can mushroom pieces
½ cup salad oil	2 tablespoons wine vinegar
½ diced green pepper	1½ teaspoons sugar
1 medium onion, chopped	1 teaspoon salt
2 garlic cloves, mashed	½ teaspoon oregano
1 small can tomato juice	fresh ground pepper to taste

Wash eggplant, remove stem, and peel or not as you choose. Cut into cubes and sauté in the oil along with onions and green pepper. Mix all other ingredients together in a bowl then add them to the eggplant mixture. Cook gently for 30 minutes. Serves four.

BUFFET GREEN BEANS

This should do for eight or nine at a buffet. It adds a certain tone to the plebian green bean.

3 packages frozen cut green
    beans or, 1½ pounds fresh,
    cut up
4 tablespoons butter
4 tablespoons flour
1 can chicken broth, heated
½ cup milk
1 teaspoon powdered thyme

Melt the butter in a saucepan, add the flour, and cook the roux gently for a few minutes. Add the heated chicken broth and the milk. Stir until the sauce is thickened and smooth. Stir in the thyme.

Cook the beans in salted water, then drain. Combine with the cream sauce, then top with the following mixture in a casserole:

1 cup herb seasoned bread
    crumbs
½ teaspoon salt
¼ cup butter or margarine
½ cup chopped pecans

Combine salt with the bread crumbs. Sauté the pecans in butter in a skillet till they are lightly browned, tossing as they toast. Add the bread crumbs to the pecans and mix. Sprinkle evenly over the beans and bake at 350°F for 25 minutes.

SMOTHERED CABBAGE WEDGES

When vegetables go sky high in the winter, here's an extremely good way to prepare cabbage. Be careful not to overcook the cabbage. It should keep its light green color and a little texture.

1 medium cabbage

Core and trim the cabbage, discarding the heavy outer leaves. Cut into 8 wedges, and cook in a small amount of salted water until just tender, 12 minutes or less. Drain well and arrange in a shallow baking dish.

The Sauce:

**¼ cup finely chopped onion
  (green if possible)
4 tablespoons butter
3 tablespoons flour
½ teaspoon salt**

**dash of fresh ground pepper
2 cups milk
½ cup mayonnaise
¾ cup grated Cheddar cheese**

Sauté onions or scallions in butter until tender, then blend in the flour, salt and pepper. Add the milk all at once to the saucepan, then cook over low heat, stirring until the sauce thickens. Pour over the cabbage wedges and bake in a 375°F oven for 20 minutes.

While it bakes, combine cheese and mayonnaise. Spoon this mixture over the top of the cabbage and bake 5 minutes more. Serves six.

LIMA BEANS CREOLE

Just as a change from succotash, try this succulent variation. Do cook the sauce down into richness—nothing is less appealing than thin tomato juice running around a plate.

3 slices bacon	1 teaspoon sugar
1 medium onion, chopped	2 cups cooked baby lima beans,
¼ green pepper, finely chopped	fresh or frozen
2 cups canned tomatoes	salt and fresh ground pepper

Sauté the bacon until crisp, then drain, crumble and set aside. In the skillet with the drippings, cook the onion and pepper until tender but not brown. Transfer to a saucepan.

Add the tomatoes and sugar, and cook the sauce uncovered until it is thickened, 15 to 30 minutes, depending on how much liquid came with the tomatoes. Stir once in a while.

Add the beans, season with salt and pepper and simmer until good and hot. Serve sprinkled with the bacon bits. Serves six.

SWEET AND SOUR ONIONS

Very interesting side dish I tasted for the first time in an Italian restaurant. This makes a pleasant change from forever creaming.

1½ pounds little white onions, or 1 package frozen (24 ounces)	salt to taste
	3 heaping tablespoons brown sugar
8 tablespoons butter	3 tablespoons white vinegar

If you use fresh onions: Peel, then boil in salted water for 5 minutes. Drain thoroughly.

If you use frozen onions: Do not cook, simply thaw on paper towels to take up the water.

Melt the butter in a large skillet and add the onions, whichever kind. Cook over moderate heat, stirring around, for about 10 minutes, until tender and golden.

Salt lightly, then add the brown sugar, mashing it into the butter, then gently stirring so that it is cooking all around the pan. Continue cooking until the onions begin to glaze, then add the white vinegar. Cook another 5 minutes until the sauce thickens and the onions are very tender. Serves four to six.

SUPER PEAS

1 package frozen peas
8 to 12 small white onions

2 tablespoons butter
salt and pepper

Peel the onions and, if they are variable in size, take a few layers off the bigger ones to make them pretty much alike. Melt the butter in the bottom of a small heavy saucepan, add the onions, cover tightly and cook over low heat for 10 minutes. Look in to make sure they aren't browning—gold is the only acceptable shade.

Turn up the heat and put the frozen peas in, season with salt and pepper and stir for 1 minute. Reduce heat again, cover, and cook about 5 minutes more until the peas are done.

Sometimes you can't get white or silver onions as they are called some places. If you use those handy frozen ones, they will cook quicker, and will need only 5 minutes of cooking before you put in the peas.

POTATO BALLS

From a lovely lady with Greek antecedents, Sophia Tarabicos, this dandy way with potatoes.

1 pound potatoes, peeled and
    cooked
¼ pound feta cheese
1 tablespoon chopped parsley
1 small onion, minced

2 eggs, separated
salt and pepper to taste
vegetable oil for frying
fine dry bread crumbs

Beat the potatoes until smooth in the electric mixer. Mash the cheese with a fork and add to the potatoes along with the parsley, onion, egg yolks, salt and pepper to taste.

Shape the mixture into tiny balls. Beat the egg whites just until foamy and dip the little balls in the whites, then in the bread crumbs. Deep fry in hot oil until golden brown. Makes 24.

THE GIANT POTATO CAKE

To go with grilled meats, ham, sausage, lots of things. Wouldn't this be great for a he-man breakfast? Easier than home fries.

3 pounds potatoes, peeled and
    grated
1 large onion, grated
½ green pepper, finely chopped
6 slices bacon

3 eggs, slightly beaten
2 tablespoons flour
1 teaspoon salt
fresh ground pepper

In processor, blender or by hand, grate the potatoes and the onion. (If you have a great deal of liquid, strain some off.) Mix in a bowl.

Sauté the bacon until crisp, crumble, and mix with the potatoes. In the drippings, sauté the green pepper briefly then pour it, drippings and all into the potato mixture.

Add the eggs, flour, salt and pepper and mix well. Turn into a greased shallow baking dish and bake for 1 hour at 325°F until the top is brown and the potatoes tender. Serves six.

GRUYÈRE POTATOES

The marriage of fine cheese with potatoes is bound to be a happy one. This is very good.

1½ cups milk
2 tablespoons butter
salt and fresh ground pepper
3 medium baking potatoes

1 teaspoon finely minced garlic
½ cup freshly grated Gruyère
  or Swiss cheese

Combine the milk, butter, salt and pepper in a medium saucepan.

Peel the potatoes and cut into ⅛ inch slices. Bring the milk mixture to a boil and add the garlic, then cook the potatoes in the milk about 15 minutes, partly covered.

Pour milk, potatoes and everything into a 1½ quart flattish baking dish. Sprinkle the cheese on top and bake in a 325°F oven until the sauce thickens and the top is golden brown. Serves four.

(The flatter the casserole, the quicker the thicker.)

POTATOES O'BRIEN

The big American favorite done handily in the oven. A marvelous accompaniment to broiled steak or any meats lacking sauce or gravy. This could do nicely in the oven when you have a cookout.

2½ pounds new potatoes, peeled, diced
1 green pepper, seeded, diced
1 big onion, finely chopped
1 tablespoons flour
4 tablespoons chopped parsley

1 cup grated Gruyère or Swiss cheese
salt, fresh ground pepper
1 cup Half and Half
2 tablespoons butter

Toss raw potatoes, green pepper and onions in a bowl. Sprinkle with the flour, parsley and cheese and toss some more. Season with salt and add pepper just lightly.

Put the mixture in an 8-cup casserole and pour over it the heated Half and Half. Dot with butter and bake about 1 hour until the potatoes are tender and the top beautifully brown. Serves four.

Make this in a fairly shallow casserole to get the maximum of the brown top. Delicious!

AUNT BETTY'S POTATO DISH

Marvelous for a crowd and fine to carry to a covered dish supper—it stays warm a long, long, time.

2 pounds frozen hash brown potatoes, thawed
1 pint sour cream
1 can cream of chicken soup (10¾ ounces)
¾ cup melted butter or margarine

12 ounces sharp Cheddar cheese, grated
1 small to medium onion, finely chopped

Combine all ingredients except potatoes in a bowl, a big one. Fold the thawed potatoes in gently, then turn into a 9 x 13 inch glass baking dish. Cover the top with:

corn flake crumbs

Bake at 350°F for 1 hour. Serves ten to twelve.

SAVOYARD POTATOES

These are made in the same way as escalloped potatoes but with beef stock instead of milk. Let them cook down well. They taste wonderful with steak.

6 cups new potatoes, sliced
large garlic clove, halved
6 tablespoons butter

salt and pepper
4 ounces grated Swiss cheese
1 cup beef bouillon or stock

Rub the bottom of a shallow baking dish with the halved clove of garlic, then spread some butter over.

Pat the potatoes dry, and arrange half the slices on the bottom of the dish. Salt and pepper lightly, then dot with butter and sprinkle half the cheese over. Repeat with the rest of the potatoes, butter and cheese.

Heat the bouillon and pour over gently. Bake at 400°F for about 45 minutes until tender and cooked down. Serves six.

POTATO CHEESE SOUFFLÉ

A spectacular and unusual soufflé in that you turn it out of the mold. Pretty fancy potatoes!

First: Butter a 6 cup soufflé dish generously. Butter a circle of wax paper and fit it in the bottom. Butter the sides. Put fine dry white bread crumbs in and cover sides and bottom with the crumbs, shaking out excess. Now:

1½ small boxes instant mashed potatoes (8 ounce size)	3 eggs
	⅛ teaspoon white pepper
¾ of the total minimum amount of liquid specified on the boxes	big pinch nutmeg or several gratings
	¾ grated Swiss cheese
1½ teaspoons salt (as specified on the boxes)	½ cup heavy cream

Reconstitute the potatoes according to package directions, adding salt but using only three quarters of the liquid called for. The mixture will be firm.

Beat the eggs, one at a time, into the potatoes. Add nutmeg, pepper, cream and cheese. Taste, and correct seasonings.

Pack the potato mixture into the prepared mold and bake at 375°F for about 1 hour. The soufflé is done when it has risen about 1 inch and is nicely browned.

To unmold, run a thin knife all around the top edge. Put a buttered serving dish over the top, then overturn, giving a small downward jerk. Peel the paper from the top, and if you feel it should be browner, sprinkle with a little cheese and briefly run under the broiler.

If the sides aren't browned enough to sustain the overturning, just serve from the kitchen—it will still be delicious. But you can get a little preview when you're unloosening the soufflé—check to make sure the sides are browned and if they are not, return to the oven for a few more minutes. You can make this in the morning and bake it at dinner time—but do bring it to room temperature first.

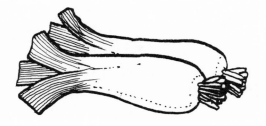

BARBADOS SWEET POTATOES

Sweet potatoes, rum and nutmeg are all indigenous to the Caribbean. They come together in this recipe which was created for a visit of Queen Elizabeth a few years back.

4 cups sweet potatoes, cooked, peeled, cut up
¼ cup dark rum
¼ cup cream
¼ cup butter

¼ teaspoon nutmeg
salt and pepper
¾ cup walnuts
grated rind of 1 orange

Put everything but the orange rind and nuts into your food processor, or combine by hand until smooth. Turn into a greased casserole. Combine chopped nuts and grated rind and sprinkle evenly over the top. Bake at 350°F for about 30 minutes when the top is crisp and golden brown. Serves four or five.

You want a good crunch in this topping. Unless you are very adept, chopping the nuts in the processor will result in ground nuts. Process in a few short bursts. For this small amount, you may want to do them by hand.

PURÉE OF POTATOES WITH HAM

Wouldn't this be good with a big vegetable plate when the garden gives up its fresh greens?

2 pounds Idaho potatoes
3 egg yolks
2 ounces butter
heavy cream

salt, white pepper
½ pound cooked ham, minced
buttered bread crumbs
2 tablespoons Parmesan cheese

Peel, cook and mash the potatoes. (Do not use the processor—they get sort of gummy.) Use the mixer and add, still beating, the egg yolks, butter and enough heavy cream to make a light, smooth purée. Season to taste with salt and white pepper.

Put some potatoes in a bottom layer of a buttered casserole. Sprinkle with ham. More potatoes, more ham and so on. Put in a 400°F oven to heat thoroughly, about 20 minutes. Then right away, sprinkle with the buttered crumbs and Parmesan. Run under the broiler to crisp and brown the top. Serves four.

RADISHES MORELIA

When you serve this, no one will really know what it is—but everyone will like it. It's from Mexico.

Wash, trim, but do not peel, as many radishes as you want for your little casserole. I used 2 packages, which served four.

Make your favorite cheese sauce, and toss some soft bread crumbs in melted butter. Set aside.

Cook the radishes in salted water until tender. Drain and combine with the cheese sauce. Turn into a small baking dish, top with crumbs and bake for about 20 minutes in a 350°F oven.

TOMATOES ROCKEFELLER

All winter we wait for them, the big, red juicy tomatoes of summer. Then it's a Niagara of firm fleshed beauties ready for your pleasure. If you have a garden, they can get ahead of you (like zucchini!), so besides making sauce for the freezer, plan to serve them often. Just the fresh slices with a little basil sprinkled over are a treat. But there are fine recipes where the tomato shines all on its own, like this one.

12 thick slices of tomato
2 packages frozen chopped
    spinach (10 ounce size)
1 cup soft bread crumbs
1 cup finely chopped onion
6 eggs, slightly beaten

¾ cup melted butter or
    margarine
½ cup grated Parmesan cheese
1 teaspoon salt
1 teaspoon thyme

Arrange the tomato slices in a lightly greased, shallow 13 x 9 x 2 baking pan. Fit them snugly.

Cook and drain the spinach according to package directions. Squeeze with your hands to get every bit of water out, then put in a bowl with all the remaining ingredients. Mix well. Spoon the mixture evenly over the tomatoes and bake for 15 to 20 minutes at 350°F until the mixture is set. Serves twelve, but makes six happier.

 Don't make this ahead. It's better baked immediately.

CREAMY SPINACH CASSEROLE

This elegant casserole has come a long way from Popeye. Sorry—no Olive Oyl.

2 packages cream cheese (3 ounce size)
2 packages frozen chopped spinach
1 cup sour cream

½ cup chopped green onions
1½ tablespoons horseradish sauce
salt and pepper to taste

Cook the spinach according to package directions, then drain in a big sieve. Press down hard to get as much water out as possible.

Blend with the softened cream cheese using a fork. Add the green onions, sour cream and horseradish combining well. Season to taste with salt and pepper. Bake in a 1½-quart casserole for 30 minutes at 350°F. Serves four to six depending on how much they like spinach.

 Take into account the great variations in commercial horseradish sauce. Some you can eat straight, others bring tears at the mention. Adjust the amount according to potency.

ZUCCHINI PUFF CASSEROLE

When you're up to here in zucchini in the summer, or want a good buffet vegetable in the winter, this one is different and very good indeed.

6 cups puréed raw zucchini, unpeeled
1 large onion, quartered
3 large eggs

1 cup grated Cheddar cheese
salt and pepper to taste
6 strips bacon, fried crisp, crumbled

Purée the zucchini along with the onion in the food processor or the blender. Get it as smooth as you can. Add the eggs to the last batch and process well. Now combine the batches in a big bowl and mix so the egg will get through it all.

Fold in the cheese and the crumbled bacon, season and turn into a greased casserole. Bake at 350°F for about 1 hour. Baking time will vary with the shape of your casserole. The puff is done when a knife inserted in the center comes out clean, and the top is puffy and lightly browned.

This is a big recipe which will serve eight. To serve four, cut it in half and use 2 small eggs. Baking time will be a little less.

RITA'S PARTY ZUCCHINI

When you have company and don't want any last minute scramble in the kitchen, here's your vegetable, ready when everything else is, prepared well ahead.

2 pounds zucchini, sliced
2 medium onions, sliced
1 stick butter or margarine
8 ounces Pepperidge Farm
   stuffing mix

1 cup grated carrot
1 cup sour cream
1 can cream of chicken soup
salt and pepper to taste

Cook the zucchini and onions in boiling, salted water for about 5 minutes, then drain well. While the vegetables drain, melt the butter in a skillet and toss the stuffing mix in it.

Mix the drained vegetables with the carrots, sour cream and chicken soup. Taste and season. Put half the stuffing mix in the bottom of a baking dish. Add the vegetable mixture, then top with the rest of the stuffing. Bake for 30 minutes in a 350°F oven when the top should be nicely browned.

You can make this with yellow squash or with half-and-half zucchini and yellow squash.

ZUCCHINI SOUR CREAM CASSEROLE

This fine recipe from a reader has an unusual quality of crisp freshness.

1 cup soft bread crumbs
6 tablespoons melted butter
1 large onion
2 pounds zucchini, trimmed
    but unpeeled

½ cup sour cream
salt and pepper to taste

If you have a food processor: Make the crumbs with the steel blade in place, then toss in the melted butter.

Rinse the bowl, then quarter the onion and process fine. Without rinsing the bowl, change to the shredder blade and shred the zucchini.

Drain all the water you can from the zucchini. Put it in cheese cloth or a tea towel and squeeze with all your might. Lots of water will come out.

Combine uncooked onions and zucchini with the sour cream. Season with salt and pepper and turn into a lightly greased casserole. Top with the buttered crumbs and bake for about 20 minutes at 350°F. Serves four or five.

Without a processor, grate zucchini by hand, chop onions fine and proceed with the recipe.

Show and Tell

People frequently ask me how my newspaper columns began. I was a feature writer before becoming a food writer, but all this was preceded by an earlier food career which might be accurately described as a plunge into a heady and terrifying media experience.

In the Fifties, when television was a mere sprout and Julia Child unknown, the number of sets in use was negligible. But Delaware did indeed get a licensed channel, NBC's Channel 7, WDEL-TV, now WHUY-TV, Channel 12, the area's public broadcasting station.

One day, my dear, good friend Gorman Walsh, who was manager of both the TV and radio stations with WDEL call letters, phoned me . He was perturbed. After weeks of searching, he had concluded that even talented Home Ec people couldn't talk it up, and the talkers couldn't cook.

"You're a good cook," he said, and then gratuitously, "and you certainly can talk!" The upshot was that I found myself committed to a daily—you did get that?—daily half hour cooking show on television.

I had never demonstrated cooking before. I had certainly never been on television. Where the chutzpah came from is still a mystery, but it seemed a good idea at the time.

When one considers today's glamorous, taped, well rehearsed cooking shows in vital color, it was all something of a miracle. I would cook the major pieces at home in the morning, assemble the ingredients to repeat on air, then drive to the station with the program on the car seat.

It was a tricky business when there was a slithery dish or a gelatin creation. While the car climbed the one steep hill with a sharp turn, I would drive with one hand, tilting the plate or container to keep it level.

After what happened on the first Cosmopolitan Kitchen Show, it is amazing to me in retrospect that I didn't go into exile immediately. I had prepared so well, timed so tightly, executed so skillfully that on the air, I finished ten minutes ahead of the end of the program.

Have you ever tried to conceive of eternity? I know what it is. Eternity is ten minutes on the big studio clock when you haven't the faintest idea of how you are going to fill those minutes.

Stricken faces in the control room, clearly visible, didn't help. The boys recognized the problem.

I talked and talked and talked. I covered French markets, English inns, made a pitch for my appliance sponsor. It was a nightmare.

Hours later, the ten minutes came to an end. A grinning Jim Adshead, who was the program director, emerged from the booth. He assured me that never, ever would I have to be frightened of television. The worst thing that could happen, had.

We survived.

Just before 2:00 P.M., Mary, who kept house for us, would line the two children up in front of the set and they would watch—with limited enthusiasm. My husband was convinced they thought everybody's mother was on TV, but they must have wondered why I was passing myself off as Eleanor Glenn.

My husband had a more vested interest. He claimed to be the only man for miles around who could look in at some bar and grill's TV set and find out what he was having for dinner.

I kept up this dizzy pace for some months, always one step ahead. But when the NBC-TV Philadelphia station offered me a talk show, I must confess I snapped it up, much as I expected to miss Jim and Jack and Charlie and Bob—all of them who were great fun.

Those were great days, but I have never demonstrated cookery again and don't plan to.

Twenty years later my second food career began, and this one I'll keep as long as you'll have me.

Egging You On...

Eggs and Cheese

My Mother was a splendid, loving, self assured woman, wonderfully at home in her kitchen but not normally given to rather poetic asides.

So I recall vividly, as a small girl, watching her cook one day. She held up an egg. "Look how beautiful it is," she said. "It's perfect."

How perfect, how functional, how versatile is apparent to me almost every day. Ingeniously constructed, the egg has a membrane system in it, holding the yolk suspended, a design contemporary engineers might envy. The yolk is further protected by a thin membrane which keeps it from mingling with the white.

But in your kitchen, it is the wide range of uses that makes the egg so desirable. It thickens your sauces. It holds your bread crumbs on whatever. It binds ingredients together. It clarifies soup, and the shells will clarify coffee.

It acts as an emulsion stabilizer in Hollandaise, mayonnaise and other sauces. It gives flavor to custards and sauces. When you bake a cake, the viscosity of the eggs when beaten causes little sacs of air to form. They don't break. When the oven heat reaches them, they balloon and make your cake rise.

Eggs behave better at room temperature than when they are cold. If you break an egg, inadvertently, it's easier to pick up the shell with a piece of shell.

Despite the claims of many citizens, brown eggs are not different from white eggs except in color.

In cooking, don't try to use half an egg. Use as small a one as you have. Never rush eggs—they want to be cooked slowly, or they harden.

Apart from all that, eggs are simply delicious eaten just as is, and the best emergency food you can keep around.

They must be good. We each eat about two hundred and sixty-five of them a year.

*　　*　　*

Clifton Fadiman once described cheese as milk's leap to immortality, a phrase I love and use often.

One fine food writer compares cheese to wine, in that it varies in relationship to milk as wine does to the grape. There are families of cheeses in special geographic locations, and while a few may be reasonable facsimiles, in other areas, not many are.

We know from early Sumerian tablets that cheese existed four thousand years before Christ. It is referred to in the Bible and crops up in the Odyssey. Cheese became known to outlying and outlandish people because it was good soldier fare for Caesar, and even Ghengis Kan.

Through the centuries, cheeses became refined and specialized in certain places and their names reflect their origins. Scandinavian cheeses, the kind I grew up with, almost always end in "ost" which simply means cheese in Norway and Sweden. Danish cheeses end with "bo" so you can earmark those easily.

Stilton comes from Stilton, and Cheddar from Cheshire in England; Limburger, Germany; Parmesan, Parma, Italy. The cheese may be named for its shape, its maker, for any number of things.

I suppose the three cheeses I use most in cooking are a sharp Cheddar, a Gruyère, and the multi-use cream cheese which plays a role in many recipes. That gives me a strong, a delicate, and a neutral, with more texture than flavor. For salads I very much like the bleus and Gorgonzola to give a nice lift to the greens. For dessert, the gentle "bo's" and melting Brie are my favorites. But everyone has his own cheese to his own taste.

Cheese adds flavor, texture and often color to foods. No home should be without it, ever.

Eggs

EGG LOAF

The person who says, "She can't even boil an egg" to put down a cook, has got her priorities wrong. Cooking eggs is a tricky business. At least, there's a foolproof way to hard cook eggs. Put the eggs in a pan with cold water that comes at least 2 inches above them. Bring the water to a boil, then turn off the heat and cover immediately. Let the eggs sit for 15 to 20 minutes, drain and run lots of cold water over. One day I forgot a pan of eggs until 30 minutes had elapsed and they were still usable. The yolks had not turned rubbery and that ominous green ring had not formed.

Sometimes you'll hit a whole batch of eggs that stubbornly refuses to give up its shells neatly. Try removing under cold running water, but if they still end up looking as though they've had the pox, don't try to devil them—go with the recipe below.

12 hard cooked eggs
⅓ cup chopped celery
½ cup chopped stuffed olives
2 tablespoons very finely
    chopped onion

1 stick of butter at room
    temperature
salt and pepper to taste

Use butter, not margarine, or your loaf will not firm up enough. Combine the soft butter with everything but the eggs and mix well. Chop the eggs as if for egg salad and fold into the mixture. Season to taste, then chill. Re-season, then form into a loaf to serve with cold meats, tomatoes and so on.

BEEF AND SPINACH SCRAMBLE

A splendid all-in-one dish that comes from Vanessi's famous restaurant in San Francisco. Fast!

2 packages frozen chopped
   spinach
4 tablespoons olive oil
4 tablespoons butter
6 green onions, chopped,
   including some green

1½ pounds ground beef
8 eggs, lightly beaten
½ cup grated Parmesan cheese
salt and pepper

Cook the spinach according to package directions, then drain and literally, with your hands, squeeze out as much water as you can.

Put half the butter and oil in a large skillet and sauté the onions until they change color slightly. Add the meat, and over higher heat sauté, breaking it up as it browns slightly. Cook until the juices are gone. Add the rest of the oil and butter, then toss the spinach with the meat in the skillet, mixing well.

With the heat somewhat reduced, pour in the eggs, add the cheese and season with salt and pepper as the eggs set. Keep loosening the eggs from the bottom of the pan and stirring the mixture. It will take about 4 minutes. Serves six.

DEVILED EGGS WITH ASPARAGUS

It looks like a formidable list of ingredients, but this interesting casserole demands only three things: you cook and cut up asparagus; you devil some eggs; you make a cheese sauce. You bake when you're ready—a dinner in a dish for eight.

1½ pounds fresh asparagus or 2
    boxes frozen
8 hard cooked eggs
1 can deviled ham, small size
    (see note)

¾ teaspoon dry mustard
2 teaspoons mayonnaise

Sauce:

4 tablespoons butter
4 tablespoons flour
2 cups milk
1 heaping cup grated sharp
    cheese

¼ teaspoon dry mustard
salt and pepper to taste

Topping:

1½ cups crushed corn flakes

2 tablespoons melted butter

Cook the asparagus till tender, then drain and cut into 2 inch pieces, removing any tough stem. Arrange in the bottom of a buttered casserole. Select a baking dish that will just hold the 16 egg halves nicely.

Peel the eggs and cut in half longways. Remove yolks and mash with the ham, dry mustard and mayonnaise. Stuff the egg whites and arrange the eggs over the asparagus keeping the layer level as you can.

Make the sauce by melting butter, stirring in the flour and cooking a few minutes. Gradually add the milk, cook and stir until thick and smooth. Add the cheese and mustard, season to taste with salt and pepper and keep over heat until all the cheese is melted. Pour over the casserole then top with the corn flakes you have tossed with butter.

Bake in a 350°F oven about 20 minutes until the top is nicely golden. If you make the dish ahead and it goes in the oven cold or at room temperature, you'll have to cook it a little longer.

 Try making your own good deviled ham. The recipe is in the index under Mrs. Beeton's Potted Ham.

SPANISH POTATO ONION OMELET, OR FRITTATA

If you order an Omelet Espagnole in most parts of Spain, you won't see a bit of tomato sauce. This potato onion filling is what will arrive, and it is not only good to taste, but really makes the omelet a meal. If you don't have salt pork, use bacon or even just bacon drippings.

1 teaspoon butter
¼ cup finely minced salt pork, pressed down
1 big onion, chopped

1½ cups cooked diced potatoes
2 teaspoons water
4 eggs, beaten

To make the omelet: Melt the butter in a skillet and cook the salt pork (or bacon) bits until they begin to go brown and crisp. Add the onions, cooking until near tender. Add the potatoes (bring up the heat, and sauté till golden brown. Drain off the fat. Put butter in your omelet pan, beat the eggs with the water, salt and pepper and make a plain omelet. At fold over time, fill with the potato mixture. Serves two generously, four adequately.

To make the frittata: Sauté pork, onions and potatoes as above, right in the omelet pan. Beat up the egg mixture and when you have drained the excess fat, pour the eggs right over the potatoes, lifting gently with a spatula to let the eggs get all through. Cook over very low heat until set. Turn to brown, or set under the broiler, if you like, to brown the top.

TUNA OMELET

This is one of those dishes you'll find you can make when, as cooks are wont to say, there's nothing in the house. Most of us have a can of tuna on the shelf, and while it won't be as rich, you can substitute a little less milk for the light cream.

1 can tuna fish (7 ounces)
2 tablespoons butter
2 tablespoons flour
1½ cups light cream

4 tablespoons grated Parmesan cheese
salt, pepper to taste

Pour the oil off the tuna fish and, in the top of a double boiler, flake the fish gently, keeping it warm over hot water.

In another saucepan, melt the butter, stir in the flour and cook this roux for a few minutes over low heat. Add the cream, stirring and cooking until the sauce is thickened, then stir in the cheese. Season. Pour over the tuna in the double boiler and keep warm.

Sauce:

2 tablespoons chopped chives
6 tablespoons butter

juice and grated rind of 1 lemon

Melt the butter in a small saucepan until it foams. Skim off the foam, then to the clarified butter left, add the chives and lemon. Keep warm.

Now make an 8 to 10 egg omelet. Spoon on the tuna filling, then fold the omelet and turn out carefully on a hot platter. Pour the butter sauce over all. Serves six.

SAUSAGE STRATA

These cheesy bread dishes with all sorts of variations are commendable for the busy cook who can make them well ahead and bake when ready.

6 slices white bread
1½ pounds bulk sausage
1 teaspoon prepared mustard
1 cup grated Swiss cheese
4 eggs, slightly beaten
1¼ cups milk

1 cup light cream
½ teaspoon salt
dash of pepper
few gratings of nutmeg
dash cayenne pepper

Trim the crusts from the bread and fit the slices into the bottom of a 10 x 16 shallow baking dish.

Brown the sausage, then drain off fat. Stir in the mustard. Sprinkle the sausage over the bread slices, then cover evenly with the cheese.

Beat the eggs in a large bowl, stir in the milk and cream and the seasonings. Pour over the sausage. Bake at 350°F for 25 to 30 minutes until lovely and goldlen. Serves six.

 If you bake this right away after mixing, do pull out the oven rack and set the casserole on it before you pour the egg mixture over. Saves spilling.

LIGHT AND AIRY QUICHE

This delicate dish is a great personal favorite and I serve it with a variety of sauces. It's just right for a Sunday night supper and if you don't want to bother with a sauce—don't. It's good without.

1 unbaked pie shell (9 inch)	fresh ground nutmeg
4 eggs, separated	6 ounces grated Swiss or
1½ cups light cream	Gruyère cheese (1½ cups)
½ teaspoon salt	

Put the unbaked shell in a 450°F oven after you have pricked it with a fork. Bake for 7 minutes and take out. Reduce oven heat to 350°F.

In a bowl, beat the egg yolks slightly and add to them the cream, salt and a few healthy gratings of nutmeg.

In the mixer bowl, beat the whites until they hold stiff peaks, then carefully fold them into the yolk mixture. Fold in the grated cheese as evenly as you can.

Turn into the pastry shell and bake in the 350°F oven for 40 to 50 minutes until a knife comes out clean from the center. Let rest for 5 minutes before cutting to serve. Serves six.

Shrimp Sauce:

1 cup small cooked shrimp, fresh or canned, drained	1 rounded tablespoon flour
	dash of salt and white pepper
3 tablespoons butter	1 cup light cream

Heat the shrimp through in the butter in a small saucepan. Blend in the flour and seasonings, then stir in the cream and cook gently until thickened. If you like dill as much as I do, you might add a bit—or whatever herb you admire. You can use diced ham for this sauce, or crab if you have some.

EGG CASSEROLE

Somewhere between a souffle and an omelet lies this quick and versatile casserole. It wouldn't surprise me if you have all the ingredients right now on hand.

4 eggs, beaten well
1 cup creamy cottage cheese
¼ cup grated sharp Cheddar
    cheese

½ teaspoon paprika
½ teaspoon salt

Beat the eggs then combine with all other ingredients. Bake in a buttered casserole for 20 to 25 minutes until puffed and golden. Serves four.

If you like, fold in before baking, some well drained cut-up asparagus, or well drained crab meat or what you have on hand. That's versatile, it is.

Cheese

AMARILLO CHEESE BAKE

I don't know where this good stuff came from but it is good. If you don't have a whole mess of cowboys to chow down, you can cut it in half and it works fine.

2 cans green chilies (4 ounce size)
1 pound grated Cheddar cheese

6 eggs
1½ cups Bisquick
1 quart milk

Butter a shallow baking dish, 12 x 7 or 8 inches. Split and seed the chilies and spread them over the bottom evenly. Cover with the grated cheese.

Beat together the eggs, biscuit mix and milk and pour the batter over the cheese. Bake at 350°F for 1 hour. Serves six.

CHEESE STRATA WITH HAM

This is a make-a-day-ahead recipe that should feed at least ten. Strata is so versatile it can go with many menus, but this one, with the ham already in, is also a great one dish meal with just a salad on the side. If you use it alone, it should do for six to eight.

12 slices white bread, crusts off
1 stick margarine, melted
12 ounces sharp Cheddar cheese, grated
6 eggs

1 quart milk
½ teaspoon Dijon mustard
1 teaspoon salt
dash cayenne pepper
2 cups ham, cubed

Cut the bread slices three ways down, three ways across, toss them in the melted margarine and arrange in a 9 x 13 casserole. Sprinkle the Cheddar over the bread cubes.

In a big bowl, whisk together the eggs, milk, mustard, salt and pepper. Add at least 2 cups of cubed cooked ham. Pour into the casserole and refrigerate, covered, overnight. Next day, bring to room temperature and bake at 325°F, uncovered for 1 hour.

CHEESE AND TOMATO PIE

Cheat on this crust and still have a fine dish full of flavor.

3 or 4 slices white bread, crusts off
butter
1 egg white, slightly beaten
4 tablespoons fine dry bread crumbs
1 can tomatoes, medium size

1 tablespoon grated onion
salt and pepper
1 teaspoon sugar
4 ounces grated Cheddar cheese
2 eggs
1 cup milk

Butter the bread slices, then generously butter a 9 inch glass pie plate. Arrange the bread slices to line the plate, butter side down. Brush the top of the bread with the beaten egg white and sprinkle evenly with the crumbs.

Drain the can of tomatoes and lay the tomato pieces on the crumbs, saving the juice for another day. Sprinkle with salt, pepper, sugar and onion. Top with the grated cheese.

Now beat together the eggs and milk and pour over all. Bake at 350°F for 30 minutes. Serves four.

The End of Abundance

In reviewing the past decade, as the Eighties begin, all of us have been brought up short by the cruel inflation and the frightening oil shortage—both heralding the end of abundance in America.

Most of us have been privileged in this land to spell out our hospitality with a groaning board, to spill out our richness from the horn of plenty, lavishly and wastefully. Our food bills have made less of a dent in our incomes than those of any peoples in the world.

Now, it's over. Now we must live with it, less meat and fish, less cheese and cream, more vegetables from the garden and the freezer, more pasta, rice and beans all around.

You can approach this dilemma with despair, or you can meet it with a new awareness in the kitchen. By using imagination and variety in preparing vegetables, by extending meat and sea food with rice or pasta, by reducing the over-generous servings of beef we usually accord ourselves, you can still offer your family good food on a regular basis.

It hurts to shop in the supermarket these days, to watch the consternation on the faces of people as they grope through the packages in the butcher's case. The only way to go is with solid planning, with clipping every coupon that promises a reduction, with menus firmly in mind, and without impulse buying except when there's an unadvertised windfall.

One way to make this dreary prospect a little more interesting might appeal to you. Years ago, when my husband and I took the two children on a protracted trip through Europe, we developed a system to hopefully keep us on our budget, but not result in day after day monotony at tables. Feeding four at a blow in restaurants can be expensive, so we always picnicked for lunch.

But for dinner, we devised Rich Days and Poor Days. Sometimes when a great restaurant or a famous regional speciality lay ahead, we would even have two Poor Days in a row. Then we would seek out the small cafe, the gast haus, the inn where we could eat simply and well, but on the cheap.

Comes the glorious Rich Day! Pick of the menu. Don't even look at the Tourist Dinner side. Tonight, we're à la carte the whole way.

You might find this thinking helpful in feeding your family since it gives you a sense of control, and does not deny your group the pleasure of an occasional splendid meal. Amusingly enough, you may soon find that the children enjoy the Poor Days more. They're big on beans!

Lately, I have heard many women say that they simply can't afford to entertain any more. That's nonsense. They mean they can't afford a filet of beef, or four pounds of crab meat or imported wine. Since everyone's in the same boat, just set your sights down and you'll soon discover that a gigantic lasagna and California wine make a great party.

One of the best dinner parties I ever had was based on a pasta dish. (In the next chapter, look for Pasta With Just About Everything.) Granted we went to the table about eight thirty, it was still immensely gratifying when one of the guests said they should be going home since it must be about eleven. It was actually one o'clock in the morning and we were still at table, having eaten all the pasta and, shall we say, more than one bottle of inexpensive wine.

Good, expensive things that brighten our favorite dishes can still be used but with a lighter hand. Cheese for sauces and gratins can be reduced slightly in quantity by using a sharper cheese. Many times, the gratin is put on top to make a crunchy crisp surface. Try sautéing small bread dice in margarine with your choice of herbs and strewing these morsels over the top instead of expensive cheese. When bacon drippings and crumbles are needed for the start of a dish, use tiny dice of lean salt pork.

Since cream, light or heavy, is an essential element in so many sauces and enriches plain food so handsomely, I would recommend an English gadget called a Bel cream maker. From 4 ounces of sweet butter and 4 ounces of milk, you can make a very rich light cream by a gentle pumping action that takes about 3½ to 4 minutes of arm work.

Since you can keep butter a long time, and you generally have milk, you can enjoy a less expensive cup of cream on demand, save money and not have to stand in the supermarket line. To make whipping cream, you simply increase the amount of butter by 1 ounce. However, I have chilled the light cream in the freezer along with bowl and beaters and whipped the light cream very successfully. You can get this device at pot and pan stores for about $12 (at this time).

But for big savings in your food budget, you will find the artful use of pasta, rice and beans the most rewarding: a big soup, your choice of many fine one dish meals and an opportunity for you to extend yourself into the cuisines of other countries which have for centuries, used less meat and more grains or pasta than we.

Something More...

Pasta, Rice, Beans and Grits

There are reputed to be five hundred kinds and shapes of pasta in Italy since every pasta maker tends to put his own mark on his own pasta.

But the big assortment you can get in your supermarket is pretty impressive, and you may find it rewarding to discover that more is there than macaroni and spaghetti.

Like the ubiquitous chicken, noodles appear in some form in almost every cuisine. In those other cultures, the pasta is the principal ingredient, garnished with some meat, fish or vegetables. We, on the other hand, regard the meat, fish or vegetable as the dish, and extend it with pasta.

From the tiny orzo to the giant shells, pasta offers you a fine base for many dishes and a chance for economy as well. With a pound of meat, you can stretch a dish to feed six at a blow. With cheese, you can create a good meatless meal.

Pasta cooking is easy—you just have to know when to stop. Al dente is what you want. It simply means there's a firmness, but not a hardness in the noodle. The only way to test is to taste. Use lots and lots of salted water, add a little oil to keep the pasta from sticking together and after 10 minutes, try the large noodles, after only 5 minutes, test the little ones.

For a while, experts were giving us the strange order: "Run cold water over the pasta to stop the cooking." This is fine for folks who like cold spahetti but otherwise, just drain well, and if you are not using it right that second, toss with a little butter to make the strands or pieces non-stick, and easier to handle.

Sauces for pasta are legion, and you may want to try others than the traditional red tomato sauce so common here. The white sauces of North Italy are superb, and you will find a most unusual sauce in the chapter ahead for a Polonaise sauce.

*   *   *

Rice is undoubtedly eaten every day by more people in the world than any other grain, and like pasta can add a great deal to your own cookery.

Long grain, converted, quick, wild, brown, they all have uses in your menu. Rice can be cooked in quantity ahead and either simply reheated or it can be frozen. Directions on packages are so explicit that you should have no problem in turning out perfect rice, whatever brand you use.

Packages of seasoning come with rices, and should be used with discretion. If you are putting the rice in a larger recipe, say a casserole, you may not want to use any or all of such seasonings. Use plain rice.

Rice can go through the whole meal, be part of every course. It gives body to soups, can be served alongside meat or fish or be an integral part of the entreé as in stuffed peppers and cabbage. There are many recipes for cold rice salads, and of course, it is a fine dessert element in puddings.

Rice is fast, easy, nutritious and good to taste which puts it up in Class A.

*   *   *

If it hadn't been for the bean, the West may never have been won. Those dried beans sustained the pioneers as nothing else, as you can tell in any Western movie. Sometimes it seems as though they ate nothing but.

Bean soup and baked beans are truly American classics, but there are lots of other ways to go. A casserole of dried limas with ham is great picnic or buffet fare. A simple dish of white beans with tomatoes, onion and garlic has a natural affinity for leg of lamb.

Dry beans are packed with protein and they're cheap. They give a fine sense of fullness to the dinner—and four ounces a serving cost you only 118 calories.

If you decide to cook them but forget to put them to soak the night before, simply cover them with water, bring to a boil and allow them to stand in the hot water for 90 minutes, then proceed with your recipe.

*　　*　　*

I didn't eat grits for a long period since the first time I had them was in a dubious roadside restaurant in Georgia where they appeared, unannounced on the breakfast plate, greasy and tasteless.

Then I discovered how good they can be with proper cooking, in casseroles with good seasonings and cheese. As a matter of fact, one of my favorite recipes features a slice of ham, mustard on top, milk around and baked. When the ham is done, pour off the milk, heap cooked grits around it, and pour over some heavy cream. Bake a little longer; then add more cream and brown lightly under the broiler. Very, very good.

In cookbooks, you may find grits listed under Hominy. Hominy, grits, it's all the same dried corn staple so big below the Mason-Dixon line.

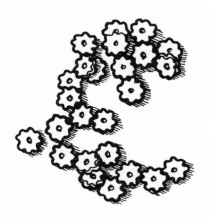

Pasta

ANNA MARIE'S WON TON LASAGNA

An Italian classic made with Chinese noodles that you hardly know are there!

Marinara Sauce:

2 tablespoons chopped onion
3 tablespoons olive oil
3 tablespoons butter
2 tablespoons chopped celery
2 tablespoons chopped carrot
1 pound lean ground beef

salt and pepper
1 cup dry white wine
½ cup milk
pinch nutmeg
3 cups Italian tomatoes

Sauté the onion in the oil and butter, then add celery and carrots and cook gently for 3 minutes. Add the ground beef, crumbling as you go, season with salt, and cook until the meat has lost its color.

Increase the heat and add the wine, cooking until the wine is evaporated. Turn the heat down, and add the milk and nutmeg and stir to combine well. Put in the tomatoes, and as soon as the mixture bubbles, turn to simmer and cook for 3 to 4 hours, uncovered, stirring occasionally. Correct seasoning at the end.

To Finish:

1 pound mushrooms, sliced
2 tablespoons olive oil
2 tablespoons butter
1 pound Chinese won ton skins

2 pounds ricotta
2 pounds whole milk mozzarella
1 cup grated Parmesan cheese
salt and pepper

Sauté the mushrooms in the oil and butter.

Layer about a quarter of the sauce in the lasagna pan. Cover with a layer of about a third of the uncooked won tons, then a layer of ricotta, mozzarella, Parmesan and mushrooms. Continue for 3 layers, ending with sauce. Sprinkle the top with Parmesan cheese and bake for 35 to 45 minutes at 350°F. Serves eight to ten.

Anna Marie sometimes adds cooked sweet or hot sausage to this recipe. Another variant is to sprinkle layers with fresh basil and parsley.

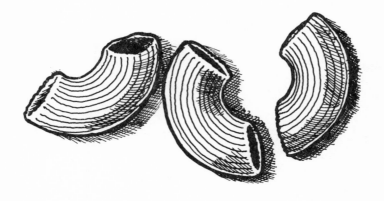

PASTA WITH JUST ABOUT EVERYTHING

This is such a big, hearty welcoming dish that it makes a success of any informal party or just endears you to your family. It will serve eight. You can do it ahead.

1 large jar store bought mari-
    nara sauce

Meatballs:

1 pound ground veal with ½
    pound ground pork
2 eggs, lightly beaten
½ cup chopped parsley
grated rind of 1 lemon
1 cup bread crumbs

4 tablespoons grated Parmesan
    cheese
½ teaspoon grated nutmeg
1 small garlic clove, finely
    minced
salt to taste

Mix everything together and shape into small meatballs. Dust with flour and brown all over in half oil, half butter. Put the marinara sauce in a pan and add the meatballs. Cook for 1 hour while you get the "Everything" ready:

2 packages frozen chopped
    spinach
1 pound ricotta cheese
3 eggs, lightly beaten

½ cup grated Parmesan cheese
¼ cup chopped parsley
2 teaspoons salt
fresh ground pepper

Cook the spinach, drain and squeeze out every bit of water you can. In a large bowl, combine spinach, ricotta, eggs, cheese, parsley, salt and pepper and the marinara sauce being careful not to break up the meatballs. Cook:

1 pound macaroni or other tube
    like pasta for just five
    minutes

Drain the pasta well and add it to the "Everything." Put into a big rather shallow baking dish and bake about 30 minutes at 375°F. Serve with grated Parmesan or Romano cheese on the side.

PASTITSIO

The great Greek buffet dish that is especially good for a party since it wants to be served lukewarm, not hot, hot. You can put this all together the day before.

1 pound elbow macaroni	dash of nutmeg
5 tablespoons butter	3 tablespoons flour
1 cup finely chopped onion	3 cups milk
1½ pounds ground round steak	¾ cup light cream
1 cup tomato purée	3 egg yolks, lightly beaten
salt and pepper	¾ cup Parmesan or Romano
¼ teaspoon cinnamon	cheese, grated
¼ teaspoon oregano	

Cook the macaroni in lots of boiling salted water until tender but firm. Drain, toss a little butter in, and set aside.

Sauté the onion in 2 tablespoons of the butter. Add the meat and brown, chopping up as you go. This will take about 10 minutes. Add the tomato purée and season with the cinnamon, oregano and nutmeg, salt and pepper.

While the meat browns, melt three tablespoons of the butter in a saucepan, add the flour and cook the roux for a few minutes. Add the milk, cooking and stirring until the sauce is smooth and thickened. Combine the egg yolks and cream in a bowl, then stir this mixture into the cream sauce, heating but not allowing to boil.

In a big rectangular or oval baking dish or a lasagna pan, layer macaroni then meat, macaroni then meat. Pour the cream sauce over all and top with the grated cheese. Bake at 375°F for 45 minutes. Let rest before serving. Serves ten to twelve.

SPAGHETTI à la FERRARA

A rich and interesting tomato sauce for pasta from a superb Italian cook, once a Ferrara.

1 pound Italian sausage
2 tablespoons oil, olive or
    vegetable
1 medium onion, chopped
1 garlic clove, chopped
⅓ cup chopped parsley

⅔ cup chicken stock or bouillon
1 package frozen peas
1 can tomatoes (8 ounces)
2 tablespoons dried basil
1 pound spaghetti, cooked
½ cup grated Parmesan cheese

Put the big kettle of water on for the pasta so that it will be ready. The sauce is quick.

In a large skillet, brown the sausage in oil, cutting at it to keep the pieces small. When browned, drain off as much fat as you can and return to the heat.

Add the onion, garlic and parsley to the skillet and sauté until the onion is tender. Add the stock, the peas and the basil and tomatoes. Cover and simmer about 5 minutes until the peas are just tender.

Meanwhile, you have cooked the spaghetti al dente. Drain it well and toss with Parmesan cheese and a bit of butter. Serve topped with the sauce and more cheese. Serves six.

MARJORIE'S SPAGHETTI

I have a dear, longtime friend named Marjorie who does not like the acid bite of tomato paste encountered in so many Italian red sauces. So over the years she developed this rich and savory sauce and kindly gave the recipe to our collection.

1 green pepper, chopped
3 medium onions, coarsely
   chopped
2 garlic cloves, minced
olive and vegetable oil
1 pound ground beef chuck
salt and pepper
1 jar Ragu spaghetti sauce
   (15½ ounces)

¾ cup dry red wine
2 tablespoons brown sugar
½ cup chili sauce
1 large bay leaf
2 teaspoons dried celery leaves
1 teaspoon basil
1 teaspoon oregano
¼ cup minced parsley

Sauté the green pepper, onion and garlic in part olive, part vegetable oil until tender. Add the meat, season with salt and good amount of pepper, and sauté till the meat loses color.

Add the Ragu sauce, wine and all the remaining ingredients. Simmer about 2 hours in a heavy saucepan—I do the whole thing in a Dutch oven—and stir once in a while. The sauce will be very rich and very thick.

Serve over any pasta that turns you on. Marjorie likes very thin spinach noodles under it. Serves six.

SPAGHETTI POLONAISE

This unusual sauce comes from Winkler's Restaurant, and it is delicate and very good. Don't worry about the pickles—it all goes together in a lovely blend.

½ cup dill pickles, julienne   ½ cup mushrooms, julienne
½ cup ham, julienne   ½ cup pimentoes, julienne

Cut into match-sticks and set aside.

3 garlic cloves, minced fine   monosodium glutamate
3 tablespoons butter   grated Parmesan cheese
1 cup brown sauce   pasta of your choice
2 cups Half and Half

Sauté the garlic in a skillet. Add the pickles and ham, continuing to sauté. Then put in the mushrooms and pimentoes, sautéing lightly. (This may be the most colorful skillet of food you will ever see.)

Stir in the brown sauce, then gradually add the Half and Half. Season with MSG and taste to see if you need salt. Simmer uncovered until the mixture thickens.

Serve over spahetti and sprinkle with Parmesan cheese.

Brown Sauce for Spaghetti Polonaise:

Restaurants keep a variety of sauces on hand. Brown sauce stock, frequently used, is based on beef bouillon simmered traditionally a long, long time, then skimmed, seasoned, and paid attention to for several days.

You can make a much quicker one for use in the Spaghetti Polonaise recipe or others that require it.

2 cups canned beef bouillon
½ cup dry white or red wine
the tip of a bay leaf
parsley sprigs

¼ cup mixed minced onions,
  carrots, celery
pinch of thyme

Simmer all ingredients for 30 minutes or so. Strain.

2 tablespoons cornstarch

Dissolve the cornstarch in a bit of cold water. Add to the bouillon and simmer for 2 to 3 minutes until thickened and clear. If you like, add 2 tablespoons of Madeira wine to enrich the flavor. Makes 2 cups.

NOODLES WITH DILL

Plain noodles are great when you have a pungent sauce or a fine cheese to complement them. But as a side dish why go plain, when with a little thought you can make them very special.

1 leek, trimmed and washed, or
  6 scallions
1 medium carrot, trimmed and
  scraped

½ pound fine or medium noodles
6 tablespoons butter
salt and white pepper to taste
1 tablespoon or more dill weed

Use only the white part of the leek, but go a little way up in the green if you use the scallions. Cut the leek and the carrot into 2 inch julienne strips, very thin, or chop the scallions.

Cook the vegetables in 3 tablespoons butter in a medium skillet. Meanwhile cook the noodles according to package directions. Drain well, then add them to the skillet. Put in the rest of the butter and the dill and toss gently. Serves four.

ANNE'S GREEN NOODLE DISH

This is so good that it should be a sin.

1 pound mushrooms	salt and pepper to taste
¾ cup butter or margarine	1 cup heavy cream
1 garlic clove	½ cup grated Parmesan cheese
½ pound prosciutto or bacon, diced	1 pound green spinach noodles

Wipe the mushrooms clean and slice them. In half the butter in a skillet, sauté the whole garlic clove until it is golden brown, then fish it out and discard.

Add the mushrooms to the skillet and sauté until they are limp, maybe 10 minutes. Season with salt and pepper.

Meanwhile be cooking the pasta in a big pot of boiling salted water just to the al dente stage. While it cooks, sauté the prosciutto in the remaining butter. (If you use bacon, you won't need that much butter.)

Now—bring the cream just to the boiling point. Drain the noodles. In a heated serving dish, toss the pasta with the mushrooms, prosciutto and the cream and Parmesan cheese. Serve immediately. Serves six.

RICH FOLK NOODLES

Rich with mushrooms and cream, this noodle dish is fine to serve with buffet, a treat for your big family when you serve grilled meat or cold ham or beef. It will serve six at table, more on a buffet.

1½ cups thinly sliced onions	1 package narrow noodles
½ cup butter	(1 pound)
2 cups fresh mushrooms, sliced	salt and fresh ground pepper
1½ cups heavy cream	

Sauté the onions in butter until they turn lightly gold. Add the mushrooms and cook till translucent. Pour in the cream, bring to a boil, then simmer very gently a few minutes to reduce the cream slightly.

Meanwhile cook the noodles in lots of water, 1 tablespoon of salt to a gallon. Don't cook to a mush—when they hit the hot cream they'll continue to cook. Drain noodles.

Combine sauce and noodles and season with salt and pepper to taste. Keep hot over hot water if you have the equipment. If you use a hot tray keep it on low. Serves six.

NOODLES ROMANOFF

Less expensive than the store bought frozen ones, this makes a dandy casserole which goes well with a surprising number of meats and vegetables.

2 packages fine or medium
    noodles (8 ounce size)
butter
2 packages cream cheese,
    softened (8 ounce size)
1 pint sour cream

⅓ cup finely minced onion
1 teaspoon Worcestershire
    sauce
1 teaspoon salt
½ cup fine buttered bread
    crumbs

Cook the noodles according to package directions, drain and put in a large bowl. Add a tablespoon or so of butter and toss to keep them from sticking together. People should stick together, not noodles.

Combine cream cheese, sour cream, onions and seasonings. Stir into the noodles, lifting gently, covering well. Pour into a 2 quart casserole and top with the bread crumbs. Bake for 25 minutes in a 350°F oven till the top is golden. Serves six.

POTATO DUMPLINGS (GNOCCHI)

4 pounds baking potatoes
    peeled, cut up
1½ teaspoons salt

1 large egg
½ cup flour, more or less

Cook the potatoes in salted water until tender. Drain, then dry thoroughly by shaking the pan over low heat. Mash to smooth consistency and let cool a little.

When the potatoes are lukewarm, beat in the egg. Add the flour a little at a time, mixing after each addition until you have a smooth elastic dough.

Turn the dough out on a floured board, pat out, then cut into pieces about the size of a Ping Pong ball. Roll these pieces into a shape like a bread stick. Cut each stick into 1 inch pieces and allow the gnocchi to rest.

Boil a very large pot of water and salt well. Put a few gnocchi at a time into the water. They will promptly sink. As soon as they rise to the surface, remove with a slotted spoon, drain and keep hot while you finish the lot.

Rice

RISOTTA

If you have never cooked rice this way, you have a great treat in store. It is impossible to give the exact amount of stock required since the rice will vary in its absorbing qualities.

3 tablespoons butter
½ cup finely chopped onions
2 cups raw long grain rice
¼ cup dry white wine (optional)
¼ teaspoon saffron

1 teaspoon salt
4 to 5 cups good chicken stock
2 tablespoons minced parsley
½ cup grated Parmesan cheese
butter

In a heavy saucepan, melt the butter and cook the onions until they are soft and golden. Stir in the rice, making sure it is well coated with the butter, and cook until it turns yellow and shiny.

Add the wine (if used), saffron and salt, and cook until the wine is absorbed. Add 1 cup of the chicken stock, cover, and cook until it is absorbed. Continue to add broth, 1 cup at a time until the rice is firm but tender. This takes a while, 20 to 30 minutes.

When the rice pleases you, stir in a dollop of butter, then the parsley and cheese. Take off the heat and let stand covered for a few minutes to let all the flavors meld. Serves six.

FRANI'S RICE

The first time I tasted this was at a buffet after Thanksgiving and it accompanied cold turkey and ham. You will find it wonderfully seasoned and textured.

1 package frozen chopped
    spinach (10 ounces)
1 cup cooked rice, white or
    brown
1 cup grated sharp Cheddar
    cheese
2 slightly beaten eggs

2 tablespoons soft butter
⅓ cup milk
2 tablespoons chopped onion
½ teaspoon Worcestershire
    sauce
1 teaspoon salt
¼ teaspoon rosemary (or thyme)

Cook spinach according to package directions. Drain well. Combine with all other ingredients and turn into a 1½ quart baking dish. Bake at 350°F for 20 to 25 minutes. Serves eight.

BROWN RICE WITH ORANGE
AND MUSHROOMS

This comes from a Florida friend. Where else? Excellent with chicken.

1 medium onion, chopped
4 ounces butter
1 cup fresh mushrooms in large
    dice
2½ cups orange juice

½ cup dry sherry
1 cup brown rice
¼ cup seedless raisins
½ teaspoon marjoram
salt and pepper to taste

In a heavy saucepan or a heavy skillet (with lid) sauté the onions in the butter until soft, then add the diced mushrooms and cook briefly.

Pour in the orange juice and sherry, bring to a boil, then add the rice, raisins, marjoram and salt and pepper to taste. Cover and cook slowly over very low heat about 50 minutes until all the liquid is taken up. Look in once in a while. The rice may be ready sooner. Serves four.

Beans

THE BIG BEAN CASSEROLE

On a cold winter night, lay this on your hungry family. It will fill eight stalwarts with great satisfaction.

1 jar B and M baked beans (1 pound, 2 ounces)	1 teaspoon salt
1 can kidney beans (15 ounces)	3 tablespoons vinegar
1 can lima beans (15 ounces)	½ cup ketchup
1 can cut green beans (16 ounces)	½ cup brown sugar
1 teaspoon dry mustard	8 slices bacon, cut into squares, not cooked
1 tablespoon Worcestershire sauce	

Drain and rinse beans. Mix everything together and bake in a casserole for 1 hour at 325°F.

That's all there is to it. Serves eight.

WHITE BEANS IN A CASSEROLE

When potatoes pall, here's a good change. This is especially delicious with lamb because of the garlic.

**1 pound small white dried
   beans**

Cook the beans according to package directions, but put an onion in to flavor. Drain and set aside.

The Sauce:

**2 tablespoons butter
1 medium onion, chopped
⅓ cup tomato purée
5 tomatoes, peeled, seeded,
   chopped or, 1 medium can,
   drained, chopped**

**3 garlic cloves, finely minced
salt and pepper
2 tablespoons chopped parsley**

Sauté the onion in the butter, then add the purée, the tomatoes, garlic, salt and pepper. Simmer about 30 minutes then stir in the chopped parsley. Stir the sauce into the beans.

Reheat in the oven when ready to serve. Serves six.

Grits

GRITS SOUFFLÉ

Plain old grits in an elegant manner!

**2 cups grits
1 package grated sharp
   Cheddar cheese
5 egg yolks**

**6 egg whites
garlic salt to taste
pepper**

Cook the grits according to package directions. Once cooked, remove from the heat and fold in the grated cheese, stirring until the cheese is completely melted. Add the egg yolks all at once and stir until blended. Season with garlic salt and pepper to taste. Let the mixture cool to room temperature.

Beat the 6 egg whites until they hold peaks, but are not dry. Gently fold them into the grits mixture and turn into a well buttered soufflé dish. Bake at 400°F for 25 minutes. Serves six.

GRITS CASSEROLE

Put four Southerners in a room and you'll get four different ways to cook grits. Here's one that could stop any controversy. If the amount of pepper scares you, start with less—you can always add. This is good with ham, Southern, country or otherwise.

2 cups dried grits	**1 tablespoon salt**
8 cups water	

Cook the grits according to package directions until thick. Turn into a big mixing bowl and add:

2 eggs	**1 cup light cream**
1 cup sharp cheese, grated	**2 tablespoons butter or bacon**
1 tablespoon black pepper	**drippings**
1 tablespoon Worcestershire	
sauce	

Mix thoroughly and pour into a baking dish. Sprinkle with paprika and bake for 1 hour or longer at 350°F. Serves eight to ten.

Party Lines

My sister Irene was at a party one night at the home of a good friend. In that little ploy we all make, she popped into the kitchen before dinner was served to ask if there was anything she could do.

In the correct response to the ploy, the hostess said no, thank you, but then amended the reply by asking if Irene would taste something for salt. In the moments the hostess was getting the something, Irene glanced down at the counter where lay a little list that said:

5:30 Casserole oven
5:40 Slice tomatoes
5:55 Water bl for rice
5:56 Go to the john
6:00 Guests arrive
6:10 Appetizers
6:30 Toss salad
       and
         so
           on

Comical, yes, but highly understandable to the party giver who lives in dread of not having everything done on time.

What you don't need at your own party is worry, and to that end, a little time table is a pretty good idea. Two more suggestions for unflustered entertaining: never serve anything you haven't cooked before, and avoid, as much as possible any last minute cooking.

When planning a menu for a dinner party, give some thought to the tastes of your guests. We all have some adorable friends who eat anything, and frequently, everything. Those are the ones I call up and ask if they'd like to come and eat the food page. They know in advance, it's a chance, that it's a test menu.

But many people simply will not eat curry. Many cannot eat shellfish because they turn ill from it. Loads of people find cucumbers more than they can digest. It's best to come right out with it unless it's a formal dinner by written invitation, in which case you have enough courses so that the guest will not go hungry.

That's principally for the main course. But as for the extra goodies, anything goes, a wonderfully seasoned side dish, an exotic appetizer, the special foods that show that you care about the diners. One reminder on the extras: don't make something and lose it in the refrigerator. I can't remember the times I've stood in the kitchen after dinner watching my hostess ruefully display a beautiful cranberry mold, or a casserole of sweet potatoes, or a plate of hors d' oeuvres that she forgot to serve. Well covered, pushd to the rear of the box, they became out of sight, out of mind. We've all been guilty.

Speaking of guilty, and in the interest of a fine dinner party, check yourself out on the following quizzes. If you answer yes to everything, you're in big trouble.

As a hostess, do you:

Pop up and down right through the meal?
Apologize for your cooking?
Urge more, more, have more, ad nauseum?
Feed your pet at the table?
Rush your guests away from the table?
Get upset when someone wants tea instead of coffee?
Clean the whole kitchen before rejoining guests?

As a guest; do you:

Arrive late?
Drink too much?
Spill?
Say "I don't eat That"?
Suggest another way to cook the entree?
Talk so much you end up eating alone?
Stay too late?

Of course you don't do any of these reprehensible things. Don't you wish They didn't?

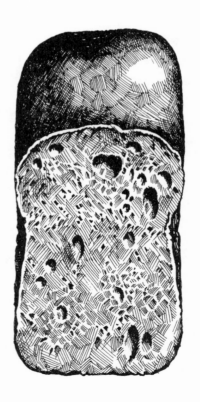

The Staff of Life...

Breads

There is a charming story about the Chinese gentleman who, right after attending an Occidental banquet, was found in his kitchen eating. He remarked how strange it was that he was always hungry soon after eating American food!

Just as we eat too little rice with a Chinese meal, he ate neither the bread nor potatoes which would have given him a more satisfied feeling.

Most people want either, and many want both. But a real bread eater wants bread on the table whatever.

Baking bread is simpler now than in the early days of our country. Imagine testing your oven by tossing in some flour, then checking the color to ascertain the temperature! The hand kneading alone, when a farm wife baked bread for a large family and the "hands," was staggering. Today with bread hooks and food processors, making a loaf of bread is a snap.

Still many people, men and women, like to make bread the old fashioned way. There is a kind of quiet pleasure in kneading which renders some contemplative and happy. Also, unless you have professional size equipment, you can only make a loaf at a time with your processor, more at a time by hand.

Most of the bread recipes herein are for baking powder breads, quick breads that you can stir up in minutes. Some of them are fruity and nutty and can easily be served as a sweet after the meal. Made into little sandwiches, they provide a fine go-along for the salad meal.

211

One of the nicest parts of baking bread, yeast or quick, is the smell of it while baking. I have always thought that the commercial put on the air a few years back by one of the giant bakeries said it with a touch of genius—"Nothin spells lovin' like something in the oven." I hope whoever wrote that was rewarded.

A to Z BREAD

This fascinating recipe won some sort of award in 1976 on the West Coast. It came into my hands from a friend returning from California. This could be one of your favorite recipes made in large loaf pans with just about anything you've got on hand, or you might make miniature loaves for small delicious sandwiches.

3 cups flour
1 teaspoon salt
1 teaspoon baking soda
3 teaspoons cinnamon
   (optional)
½ teaspoon baking powder

3 eggs
1 cup vegetable oil
2 cups sugar
2 cups A to Z ingredient
3 teaspoon vanilla
1 cup chopped nuts

Sift dry ingredients together and set aside. Beat the eggs in the large mixer bowl, add oil and sugar, and cream thoroughly.

Add 2 cups of whichever A to Z ingredient you choose. Add vanilla, then fold in dry ingredients. Mix well, then add nuts. Spoon into 2 large, well-greased loaf pans and bake for 1 hour at 325°F.

A to Z: Use one of the following or a mixture to equal 2 cups, except where indicated.

Apples, grated
Applesauce
Apricots, chopped
Bananas, mashed
Carrots, grated
Cherries, pitted, chopped
Coconut, fresh, ground
Dates, pitted, finely chopped
Eggplant, ground up
Figs, finely chopped
Mincemeat
Oranges, chopped
Peaches, peeled, chopped

Pears, chopped
Pineapple, crushed, well drained
Prunes, chopped, (use only 1 cup)
Pumpkin, canned purée
Raisins
Raspberries
Rhubarb, finely chopped
Strawberries
Sweet potato, grated
Yogurt, plain or flavored
Zucchini, grated, well drained

O'HARA BANANA BREAD

One bowl, one loaf pan, and you have super-quick banana bread. So good with fruit salad, much favored by the lunch box crowd, too.

¼ cup butter
1 cup sugar
2 eggs

3 medium bananas, very ripe
1½ cups flour
1 teaspoon baking soda

Cream butter and sugar, beat in eggs and bananas. Beat or stir in flour and baking soda. Turn into a greased loaf pan and bake for 1 hour at 350°F.

OVEN BUTTERED CORN STICKS

Easily made, and without a mold.

4 tablespoons melted butter	1 can cream style corn
2 cups Bisquick	(8½ ounces)

Melt the butter in a 15 x 10 x 1 inch pan.

In a bowl combine Bisquick and corn, stirring until they make a soft dough. Turn out on a floured board and knead about 15 strokes.

Roll out to a 6 x 10 inch rectangle, then cut into 1 x 3 inch strips. Roll the strips in the melted butter, then arrange on the buttered pan in a single layer.

Bake at 450°F for 10 to 12 minutes. Makes twenty sticks.

DILLY CASSEROLE BREAD

This recipe won top prize in a sometime ago baking contest but it is good for repetition.

1 package active dry yeast	1 tablespoon butter
¼ cup warm water	2 teaspoons dill seeds
1 cup cottage cheese, large curd	1 teaspoon salt
2 tablespoons sugar	¼ teaspoon baking soda
1 tablespoon instant minced onion	1 egg
	2¼ to 2½ cups sifted flour

Sprinkle the yeast over the warm water to dissolve. Heat the cottage cheese to lukewarm, then combine in a mixing bowl with sugar, onion, butter, dill, salt, baking soda, egg and yeast. Mix well.

Add the flour, a little at a time to make a dough, a stiff batter, beating well after each addition. Cover cosily and let rise in a warm place until doubled—1 hour or so.

Stir down with 25 vigorous strokes then turn into a well-greased 1½ quart round casserole (8 inch). Cover and let rise again for 30 minutes or until light.

Bake at 350°F for 40 to 50 minutes. If the top browns too soon, cover with foil.

FLUFFY DUMPLINGS WITH CHIVES

There is nothing as dispiriting as a soggy dumpling. In my search for a lighter than air one, this is the winner. You can vary the seasoning and use parsley or herbs, even a little sharp grated cheese but you'll find the results delicious.

2 cups sifted flour	**4 tablespoons chopped chives**
3 teaspoons baking powder	**¼ cup shortening**
1 teaspoon salt	**1 cup milk**

Sift the flour again with the baking powder and salt into a bowl. Add the chives.

Cut the shortening in with a pastry blender until the mixture is like cornmeal. Add the milk, lightly, stirring with a fork to make a soft dough. Stir as little as possible.

Drop the dough by tablespoons on top of the meat or vegetables in your stew—not into the liquid. Cook slowly for 10 minutes, uncovered. Then cover, and cook 10 minutes more. (Using a Dutch oven or any dome lidded pot helps.) This makes twelve large tender dumplings.

MOTHER-IN-LAW CINNAMON ROLLS

A family recipe. It is claimed that ten years of experimenting went into perfecting the glaze, a contention you may accept or reject!

¼ cup sugar
1 teaspoon salt
¼ cup soft margarine
½ cup scalded milk
1 package dry yeast
½ cup warm water

3¾ cups all purpose flour
1 egg at room temperature
soft butter
brown sugar
cinnamon

In a large bowl, combine sugar, salt, margarine and hot milk. Dissolve yeast in a half cup of warm water.

When the milk mixture is lukewarm, add the yeast mixture, the egg, and half the flour. Gradually add the rest of the flour, mixing until the sides of the bowl come clean. Remove from bowl and knead for 3 minutes on a lightly-floured board. Grease the dough on all sides and put back in the bowl to rise for 90 minutes.

Punch down the dough, knead again briefly, then let rise for another 15 minutes. On a floured board, roll out to a 12 x 15 rectangle. Spread with butter, then sprinkle with brown sugar and cinnamon to your liking. Roll up firmly and slice into 18 pieces.

The Famous Glaze:

1 cup brown sugar
4 tablespoons hot water

6 tablespoons cold margarine
pecans, if you like

Bring the brown sugar and hot water to the boil in a small saucepan. Add cold margarine and heat until it is totally melted. Dribble (or drizzle) into 2 greased round or square cake pans, then sprinkle it with pecans if you choose. Arrange the dough slices over, and bake at 350°F for 20 to 25 minutes. Turn out and enjoy.

ENGLISH MUFFINS MELBA

You might enjoy these more with soup than you enjoy the everlasting crackers with soup.

English muffins   optional herbs
butter

Holding each muffin firmly with the flat of your hand on a cutting board, slice through horizontally to make 3 or 4 slices, paper-thin.

Place on cookie sheets and bake in a very slow oven—200°F— for about 20 minutes. Take out, butter each slice and return to the oven for 10 more minutes. If you like, sprinkle with herbs when you butter.

HUSH PUPPIES

Long ago when frontier folk were fixing corn bread in the skillet over an open fire, this wonderful name came to be. Bits were thrown to the dogs to quiet their howling. To many Southerners, they are a must with fried fish.

1½ **cups corn meal**	1 **teaspoon salt**
¾ **cup flour**	1 **large egg**
2 **teaspoons double acting**	1 **cup buttermilk**
baking powder	1 **teaspoon onion juice**
⅓ **teaspoon baking soda**	1 **medium onion, grated**

Sift the flour, baking powder, soda and salt together and add the cornmeal. Beat the eggs slightly with the buttermilk and onion juice, then stir into the dry ingredients, mixing well. Add the grated onion and stir again.

Drop by tablespoons into hot fat in which fish has been fried. Enough puppies for six.

You don't absolutely have to fry fish to make these. Fry in vegetable oil, lacking the fish.

OATMEAL BREAD

This makes excellent toast, this good brown loaf. It came from Georgette Cole, and on the card was this legend: "From Mom, Nov. 1970, to her from Lynn Jones, Oct. 1962, to her from her mother-in-law." All of that makes a time tested successful recipe. Makes three loaves.

1 cup quick oats	½ cup warm water
2 cups boiling water	2 cups milk
4 to 5 tablespoons margarine	2 teaspoons salt
or butter	10 cups flour, approximately
1 cup brown sugar	4 of these whole wheat
2 packages yeast	salad oil

Cook oats in boiling water for 5 minutes. Stir in butter and brown sugar, and let cool to lukewarm.

Soften the yeast in the warm water and stir it into the cereal. Mix in milk and salt.

Sift the flour and stir in, a cup at a time until you have a manageable dough. Turn the dough out on a floured board and knead lightly for 3 or 4 minutes. Shape into 3 large or 4 smaller loaves and place in well greased pans.

Brush the loaf tops with salad oil, then cover and let rise in a warm place until they are doubled in bulk. Bake at 350°F for 45 minutes. When the loaves come out of the oven, brush tops with butter or margarine to keep the crust soft.

PEANUT BUTTER BREAD

I think this must have been devised during that political era when everybody pounced on Jimmy Carter's peanuts.

2 cups unsifted flour (lightly measured, not packed down)
3 teaspoons baking powder
½ teaspoon salt
½ stick butter or margarine, softened
¾ cup chunky peanut butter, room temperature
¾ cup sugar
1 large egg
1 teaspoon vanilla
1 cup milk

In a bowl, stir together the flour, baking powder and salt.

In another bowl, beat together the peanut butter and soft butter until well blended. Beat in sugar, egg and vanilla.

Add the flour mixture and, with a pastry blender, cut the flour in until fine crumbs are formed. Add the milk and stir until just moistened.

Turn into a 9 x 5 x 3 inch, well-greased loaf pan. Bake at 350°F for 55 to 60 minutes. When the top is golden brown, test in the center for doneness.

Cool on a rack. Although it will freeze well, you probably won't get a chance before it's all gone.

M.E.'s IRISH SODA BREAD

3 cups sifted all purpose flour
⅔ cup sugar
3 teaspoons baking powder
1 teaspoon baking soda
½ teaspoon salt
1 cup raisins
2 eggs, well beaten
1¾ cups buttermilk
2 tablespoons melted butter

Sift all dry ingredients together 3 times. Stir in the raisins, coating them well.

In a separate bowl, beat the eggs with a whisk, then add the buttermilk and the melted butter, whisking by hand or beating at low mixer speed. Pour the egg mixture over the sifted dry ingredients and stir until just moistened, being certain that all the flour is incorporated.

Bake in a greased 9 x 5 loaf pan at 350°F for 60 to 70 minutes. Do not underbake. If the top browns too soon, cover with foil and continue baking.

RHUBARB BREAD

A springtime specialty since you must use fresh rhubarb. This is from Sister Sienna Ehlen, a teaching nun.

1 egg
1½ cups brown sugar
¾ cup vegetable oil
1 teaspoon vanilla
2½ cups sifted flour
1 teaspoon baking soda
1 teaspoon salt

1 cup sour milk
1½ cups raw rhubarb, finely
    diced
½ cup finely chopped walnuts
½ cup sugar
1 tablespoon butter

Combine the egg with brown sugar, oil and vanilla and beat until smooth.

Sift the flour with the soda and salt. Add to the egg sugar mixture alternately with the sour milk, beating after each addition.

Stir in the rhubarb and nuts and turn the batter into two greased loaf pans, 8½ x 4½ x 2½.

Crumble the sugar and butter together and sprinkle over the loaves. Bake at 325°F for about 1 hour, until lightly browned. Cool on racks.

LORRAINE'S SQUASH BREAD

From Lorraine's aunt in Laurel, Delaware, at whose house Lorraine says you can gain 5 pounds on a weekend visit.

3 eggs
2 cups sugar
1 cup vegetable oil
2 cups grated yellow squash
3 teaspoons vanilla
3 cups flour

1 teaspoon salt
1 teaspoon baking powder
1 teaspoon baking soda
3 teaspoons cinnamon
1 cup chopped walnuts

Beat the eggs until foamy then add sugar, oil, squash and vanilla. Mix well. Combine flour, salt, soda, baking powder and cinnamon and add to the egg mixture. Stir until well-blended, then add the nuts.

Pour into 2 buttered loaf pans, 9 x 5 x 3 size, and bake in a 350°F oven for 1 hour. This moist, nutty loaf freezes well.

ROLLED CURRIED TOASTS

To go with soup, salad or, in a pinch, drinks.

½ cup soft butter or margarine　　**melted butter**
curry powder to taste　　**18 slices soft white bread**

Using ordinary supermarket bread, trim the crusts and with a rolling pin, roll each slice out very thin. Season the soft butter with curry powder to your taste, then spread each slice of bread.

Roll the slices up jelly roll fashion and secure with toothpicks. Brush a baking sheet with melted butter, then brush each curry roll with butter as you arrange them on the sheet. Bake at 350°F until lightly browned. Turn once. The bottoms will brown faster than the tops.

The Ubiquitous Sandwich

Lord Sandwich was playing cards. The stakes were high, the play was lively, and he didn't want to stop. But being hungry, he sent out for some meat, and asked that it be covered, both sides, with slices of bread so that he would not mark up the cards.

That was how it started. The French took it up, the English created another version, and the Scandinavians turned it into an art form.

But nowhere in the world did the sandwich come to dominate the culture (as well as the landscape) as it did in the United States. Everywhere you look, there is a golden arch, or a Southern colonel, or a smiling cowboy, all representing billions of dollars of annual revenue from that self same sandwich.

The hamburger (Hamburg, Germany) and the weiner, (Vienna, Austria) are the cornerstones of life to many, especially adolescents. By the way, the hot dog roll came into use around the turn of the century in somewhat the same manner as Lord Sandwich's bread. A sausage peddler in St. Louis is reputed to have offered his buyers white gloves to keep fingers clean when eating his sausages, street-side. So many walked away with the gloves, that he began putting the sausages in rolls.

Most of us eat several sandwiches a week, burg, ham, BLT, grilled cheese, club or tea. Some folks seem to survive on them, devotees of the cult of fast food.

British sandwiches are on the whole, not as interesting as ours. They don't say they are going to make a sandwich, but that they are going to cut a sandwich.

Generally, the sandwich is on perfectly square, rather thin bread, cut small for their specialties, cucumber or watercress, served larger with sometimes unusual things like baked beans.

If you go into a cafe in France and ask for a sandwich, they generally proffer ham. Now the hard, long roll is delicious. The pale pink ham is exceptional. But the sandwich is a jawbreaker, and the ham one could read through. They simply would not comprehend a deli creation with two inches of paper thin hot pastrami.

But in Scandinavia, particularly in Denmark, the sandwich is superb. Always open faced, it may be a small square of meat or sea food or eggs. If it is of shrimp, there may be twenty tiny shrimp in rows. If it is a small piece of roast beef, it is garnished with several colors of other foods.

These creations are eaten with a knife and fork, and they are anything but fast food. You want to dwell on them, look at them, savor them. In Copenhagen, you can go to a smorrebrod shop and buy them by the box to take home. One night, my husband and I bought a box after the theater, went back to the hotel, and had a gorgeous picnic at midnight.

To the end of her life, my Mother rejected the two slice sandwich. "All that bread!" she would say. She wanted the crusts off, and the spread even, all over. Her contempt for the sandwich maker who put a dollop of tuna salad in the middle, leaving the sides bare, was limitless. I must agree when I bite into a drug store counter sandwich.

The sandwich supper can be very good indeed. It might be soup, salad and sandwich, or a sturdy hot roast beef. When you grill outside it may be a steak or a hamburg.

Buf if your children carry a lunch, your husband eats a sandwich at his desk, and your adolescents meet at McDonald's, maybe you should widen their world of an evening.

A Piece of Cake...

Cakes and Cookies

When I was growing up, the Swedish Methodist Episcopal Church was the focal point of much of my family's activity.

A little church in a small town, it had been literally created by my Mother and Father along with relatives and friends who had come to this country at the same time, around the turn of the century.

What has this to do with cakes? Well, you never saw anything like the cakes that appeared at the monthly meetings of the Ladies' Aid Society of our church. Apprised of these meetings, I would saunter by after school, and with some innocent pretext, invade the Sunday School room where the meetings were held. That room adjoined the kitchen where all the good stuff was.

I was in pretty good shape because my Mother was President. Who would have denied me a piece of cousin Eleanor's black-as-ink devil's food, or Mrs. Carlson's angel food, towering and light? I was too innocent to think about it then, but now I realize it was a great competition, everyone trying to outdo the other to the benefit of many.

Do you remember seafoam icing? It was very big then, blonde and rich, and the Seven Minute was inches deep. Of course, there were spritz and hermits and pepparkokar, fine cookies but not 1-2-3 with the super cakes.

I do believe that spirit of competition still exists among the great cake bakers. When someone calls in the interest of a benefit, who could resist when they say, "Will you make your marvelous whatever cake?" You can get famous with a cake, believe me.

Many women like to bake cakes better than anything. Even though I get my big kicks from entrees, I still feel a surge of emotion when a cake goes higher and higher and I know all is well. And when it turns out on the rack docile, all in a piece, and doesn't drop perceptibly, it gives one a fine sense of mission accomplished.

Back to business: Read the cake recipe most carefully. Regular or cake flour? Sifted, or sifted twice?

Eggs at room temperature. Beaten until yellow and light. Beaten till stiff but still shiny. These little asides are terribly important.

Folding. The careful slicing through, melding the mixture without destroying the airiness.

Expectations: When it's a cake, it will rise. When it's a torte, it will be rather flat. Not to worry, that's right.

Gently, always gently with a cake.

Come to think of it, that's a pretty good general rule.

Cakes

BETTY'S APPLE CAKE

½ cup butter at room
   temperature
2 cups sugar
2 eggs
2 cups flour
1 teaspoon baking powder
pinch of salt

1 teaspoon baking soda
1 teaspoon cinnamon
5 baking apples, peeled, cored,
   sliced thin
1 cup chopped walnuts or
   pecans

Cream butter and sugar together. Add eggs and beat well in the electric mixer. Sift the dry ingredients together and add to the creamed mixture, beating until smooth.

Fold in the apple slices and the nuts, distributing them as evenly as possible in the heavy batter. Turn the mixture into a buttered 9 x 9 inch cake pan and bake at 350°F for 45 to 60 minutes. Jucier apples will keep the cake moister and require longer baking. Test at 45 minutes but leave in the oven until firm with a nice amber crust.

RITA'S DEVIL'S FOOD CAKE

Talk about easy. Talk about good. This black-as-ink devil's food cake is almost as quick as a box cake and has all the qualities we admire—it's big, it's moist and as good a cake as I have ever tasted.

2 cups all-purpose flour
2 cups sugar
2 eggs
½ cup vegetable oil
¾ cup cocoa
1 scant cup boiling coffee with
    2 teaspoons baking soda
    mixed in (See note)

1 teaspoon baking powder
1 cup milk
1 teaspoon vanilla
pinch of salt

Put everything in the big mixer bowl together. Beat at medium speed for a few minutes until everything is well combined. Pour into a buttered 9 x 13 inch cake pan, or 3 layer pans. Bake the flat cake 30 to 40 minutes at 350°F, the layers 25 to 30 minutes. Test, in any case. Ice as you choose.

When you mix the baking soda into the boiling coffee, hold the cup over the bowl. It foams and runs all over. If you like, put the boiling coffee into a bowl and add the soda.

O'HARA CHOCOLATE CAKE

2 sticks margarine
½ cup cocoa

1 cup water

Combine in a saucepan and bring to a boil while you beat together:

2 cups sugar
2 cups flour
1 teaspoon salt
2 teaspoons vanilla

1 teaspoon baking soda
½ cup buttermilk
2 eggs

Pour the hot chocolate mixture into the batter. Beat by hand until well mixed. Bake in a well greased 9 x 13 cake pan for 30 to 35 minutes in a 350°F oven. Ice with chocolate frosting or Seven Minute icing.

MADAME X's CHOCOLATE CAKE

When this appeared in the paper, it was nameless only because I agreed not to use the name of its creater—hence, Madame X. This is an excellent cake.

¼ pound butter
4 squares bitter chocolate
1 cup water
2 cups sugar
2 cups flour

1¼ teaspoons baking soda
1 teaspoon salt
2 eggs
1 cup sour cream
1 teaspoon vanilla

Melt together the chocolate, butter and water.

Sift together the sugar, flour, baking soda and salt in the big mixer bowl. Add the chocolate mixture to the bowl.

One at a time, add the eggs, beating well after each. Add the sour cream and vanilla. Turn into a greased and floured Bundt pan—not the great big one, the medium size, says Madame X—and bake at 350°F for 1 hour.

Allow the cake to remain in the pan for 15 or 20 minutes when it comes out of the oven. Turn out and serve when still slightly warm.

OATMEAL CAKE

You will be amazed at how quickly you can get this in the oven with only your good right arm to help, just like a Nebraska farm wife, long ago.

1¼ cups boiling water
¼ cup margarine

1 cup quick cooking (not instant) oatmeal

Mix the above ingredients and allow to stand 20 minutes. Now add:

1 cup white sugar
1 cup brown sugar
2 eggs, slightly beaten
1⅓ cups all purpose flour

1 teaspoon baking soda
½ teaspoon nutmeg
1 teaspoon cinnamon

Mix well by hand, then turn into a greased 9 x 15 inch pan, and bake for 25 minutes at 350°F. (If you only have a 9 x 13 inch pan, leave it in 5 minutes longer.)

While the cake is still hot, strew over the top, then spread evenly the following mixture:

6 tablespoons butter
½ cup sugar
½ teaspoon vanilla

1 cup pecans, chopped
1 cup coconut (3½ ounce can)

Put the cake under the broiler after you have put the topping on and watch while it turns golden brown. Don't leave it—it will turn very quickly.

BETTY'S HAZELNUT CAKE

Some like it hot—but not hazelnuts. They deteriorate in the summer months, and are almost impossible to buy then. So either plan this for cold (or at least cool weather) or stock up on hazelnuts when you see them and pop in the freezer. This is worth a little trouble, believe me.

6 eggs, separated	¾ cup sugar
1 whole egg	⅓ cup fine white bread crumbs
1 cup ground hazelnuts	1 tablespoon flour

In the big mixer bowl, beat the egg yolks and the whole egg until thick and pale lemony yellow. Gradually beat in the nuts, ½ cup sugar (mind it now, not the whole ¾ cup!), and the bread crumbs. Beat until the mixture forms a dense, moist mass.

In a separate bowl, beat the egg whites until they foam. Gradually add that remaining ¼ cup of sugar, continuing to beat until the egg whites hold stiff peaks.

With a rubber spatula, fold a quarter of the egg whites into the egg yolk mixture. Sprinkle the flour over gently, then fold in the remaining whites until no traces remain. A delicate touch here.

Butter and flour a 10 inch spring form pan. Turn the batter into it, smoothing the top with your spatula. Bake in the middle of the oven for 1 hour at 300°F or until the cake comes away from the sides of the pan. Be sure to test.

When you take the cake out of the oven, remove the sides of the pan immediately. Let the cake cool, then split it horizontally into two layers. Careful, it will be moist.

apricot preserves	1 cup heavy cream

To finish the cake, spread a layer of jam to make a filling between the layers.

Whip the cream, adding a tablespoon of confectioners sugar and a teaspoon of vanilla. Now spread the cream lavishly over the whole cake like a thick frosting. Strew the hazelnuts evenly over all and serve with delight.

 The cake will fall about 1/3 once out of the oven. Don't fret. It's supposed to. It's really a torte.

SOUTHERN POUND CAKE

The reader who proffered this recipe sent a note: "This cake is definitely worth the guilt feelings of the diet conscious!"

1 stick margarine
1 stick butter
½ cup Crisco
3 cups sugar
5 eggs
1 cup milk

3 cups all purpose flour
1 teaspoon baking powder
2 teaspoons vanilla or 1
    teaspoon vanilla and a pinch
    of mace

In the large mixer bowl, cream together the margarine, butter, Crisco and sugar. Beat in the eggs, 1 at a time. Add the milk alternately with the flour and baking powder. Stir in vanilla.

Pour the batter into a tube or Bundt pan, well greased, and put into a cold oven. Set immediately at 325°F. Bake for 1 hour and 15 minutes then test for doneness. Bake another 15 minutes if needed. Cool slightly before turning out.

LEMON POUND CAKE YOLANDA

A big, moist cake with a bright zing of lemon.

2½ cups all purpose flour
1½ cups sugar
3 teaspoons baking powder
½ teaspoon salt

¾ cup orange juice
¾ cup vegetable oil
2 teaspoons lemon extract
4 eggs

Glaze:

1½ cups confectioners sugar   ½ cup lemon juice

Generously butter and flour a 12 cup tube pan, regular or non-stick. Spoon the flour lightly into the measuring cup and level off. In the large mixer bowl, combine all the cake ingredients and beat for 3 minutes at medium speed. Pour into the prepared pan.

Bake at 325°F for 40 to 50 minutes until a tester comes out clean. Remove the cake from the oven but leave it in the pan.

With your long tined kitchen fork, pierce the cake deeply about every inch. Blend the glaze ingredients, and spoon just half the glaze over the hot cake. Let stand for 10 minutes. Invert on a plate and spoon remaining sauce over without piercing. Serves twelve.

WILLIAMSBURG ORANGE WINE CAKE

This is reputed to be the original recipe for the cake we can now buy commercially frozen. Good stuff.

2 oranges, grated rind only
1 cup raisins, finely chopped
½ cup walnuts, coarsely
    chopped
1 stick butter or margarine
1 cup sugar

2 eggs
2 cups flour
1 teaspoon baking soda
½ teaspoon salt
1 cup buttermilk
1 teaspoon vanilla

In the processor, or however, grate the rinds of the 2 oranges. (Squeeze the 2 oranges and drink the juice—good for you. Better, make an orange and onions salad.)

Combine half the rind with the chopped raisins and walnuts. (If you put dried out raisins in the processor it sounds like World War II, but they do get chopped.)

In the big bowl of your mixer, cream butter, add sugar gradually and beat smooth. Beat in the eggs, one at a time, with vigor. Stir in the rind-raisin-nut mixture and a teaspoon of vanilla.

Sift the dry ingredients together, and add to the butter, alternately in thirds with the buttermilk. Pour into a well greased 9 inch square cake pan, or even a spring form. Bake for 40 minutes or until it pulls away from the sides. Do test this cake, it may want a few minutes longer.

Sherry Icing

⅓ cup butter or margarine
the rest of the orange rind

2 cups confectioners sugar
sherry

Cream butter till soft, mix in sugar and orange rind then add just enough sherry to make it spreadable. Ice the top of the cake after it is cooled.

PEACH TORTE AILEEN

One of the most wonderful things that can happen to a sweet ripe peach is to end up in this superb dessert. The two layers of meringue give it a pastry chef elegance.

The Batter:

½ cup butter
½ cup sugar
4 eggs yolks, beaten
4 tablespoons milk

⅔ cup flour
1½ teaspoons baking powder
⅛ teaspoon salt

Like the pastry chef, you beat this by hand. Cream the butter and sugar, then add beaten egg yolks, milk, flour, baking powder and salt. Beat by hand 300 strokes. There is very little batter so when you spread it in two 9 inch layer cake pans, it won't look like much. Grease only the bottoms of the pans, not the sides.

The Meringue:

4 egg whites
1 cup sugar

finely chopped nuts

Beat the egg whites until foamy, then gradually add the sugar, beating until the whites hold stiff peaks. Spread the meringue over each cake layer, then sprinkle with the chopped nuts.

Bake in a 325°F oven for 25 minutes until the tester comes out clean. The meringue should be quite dry. Cool the layers slightly, then remove from the pans onto waxed paper. Leave one layer meringue side down, but turn the other so the meringue side is up while they finish cooling.

To Assemble:

Fresh peaches: Slice enough to make a thick filling between layers. Cream: Whip heavy cream, 2 cups, with a bit of sugar and vanilla. Put the bottom layer on a plate with the meringue down. Spread with whipped cream (or Cool Whip). Cover the cream with peaches, then cover the peaches with cream.

Put the top layer on, meringue side up. Frost the sides of the tort with cream, not the top. Refrigerate. This tort can be made a day ahead.

 If Cool Whip is used, get a large container.

PUMPKIN CAKE

A big, hearty, welcome-home kind of cake that stays fresh for a long, long time.

2 cups sugar
1¼ cups vegetable oil
1½ cups pumpkin purée
4 eggs
3 cups flour
2 teaspoons baking powder
2 teaspoons baking soda

2 teaspoons cinnamon
1 teapoon salt
½ cup seedless raisins
½ cup golden raisins
1 cup chopped walnuts or pecans

Put sugar, oil and pumpkin in your big mixer bowl. Beat well at medium speed. Add eggs, 1 at a time, beating well after each addition.

Sift together the flour, baking powder, baking soda, cinnamon and salt, then fold into the batter until all traces of the dry ingredients disappear. Stir in the raisins and nuts.

Bake in a well greased tube pan for 1 hour and 15 minutes at 350°F, (don't open the door and test for at least 1 hour). Cool before turning out on a cake rack. This makes twelve generous slices.

HILLIARD PRUNE CAKE

Unbelievably moist and tender, this cake is first cousin to pudding!

3 eggs
1½ cups sugar
1 cup vegetable oil
1 cup buttermilk
2 cups flour
½ teaspoon salt

1 teaspoon allspice
1 teaspoon cinnamon
1 teaspoon baking soda
1 cup chopped, cooked prunes
1 cup pecans

In your electric mixer, beat the eggs well, add sugar and continue beating, gradually adding the oil and buttermilk to make a smooth mixture.

Reduce speed to low and add the dry ingredients, which have been sifted 3 times. Note: 3 siftings. Fold in the prunes and the nuts and spread the batter smoothly in a 9 x 13 x 2 inch greased cake pan. Bake at 350°F for 40 minutes.

While the cake bakes, make a sauce of:

½ stick margarine
½ cup buttermilk

1 cup sugar
½ teaspoon soda

Put all these ingredients in a saucepan and bring to a full rolling boil. When the cake comes out of the oven, poke it full of holes with a skewer and spoon the mixture over all.

This one gets better as it gets older—like us.

RUM CAKE

A very old recipe from Maryland's Eastern Shore.

4 eggs	**2 teaspoons baking powder**
1 cup sugar	**1 teaspoon salt**
2 cups flour	

Beat eggs and sugar together, then add the 2 cups of flour you have mixed with the baking powder and salt. Beat well.

Pour into a greased tube pan and bake at 350°F for 25 to 30 minutes until it tests done.

Rum Glaze:

1½ cups sugar	**¾ cup rum**
¾ cup water	

Cook the sugar and water together until the syrup is thickened. Add the rum—the dark rum is more flavorful. Keep the syrup warm until used.

When the cake is done, turn it out on a large serving plate and slowly pour the syrup over it until the cake has absorbed it all. Cool.

When ready to serve, slice and top with whipped cream, or ice the whole top with whipped cream. Serves twelve.

RUM CAKE WITH PECANS

Almost everyone has this excellent recipe developed by guess who—a rum distiller. Anyhow, here it is in a book and you can get rid of another clipping.

1 cup chopped pecans
1 package yellow cake mix
1 package instant vanilla
    pudding mix

4 eggs
½ cup cold water
½ cup vegetable oil
½ cup dark rum

Grease and flour a 10 inch tube pan or 12 inch Bundt pan. Sprinkle the chopped pecans evenly over the bottom.

In your big mixer bowl, combine all the rest of the ingredients. Mix well on medium speed, then turn into the pan. Bake at 325°F for 1 hour, then cool before inverting on a serving plate. Prick the top all over with your 2 tine cooking fork, and drizzle the glaze over, using it all.

Glaze:

¼ pound butter
¼ cup water

1 cup sugar
½ cup dark rum

Melt butter in a small saucepan, then stir in sugar and water. Boil 5 minutes, stirring constantly. Remove from heat and stir in rum.

QUICKIE ICING

The box cake is almost ready to come out of the oven. The children will be home from school in ten minutes. Here's the fastest icing ever to meet the occasion.

1 box confectioners sugar
1 stick margarine
2 tablespoons Crisco

¼ cup boiling water
1 teaspoon vanilla

Beat it all together until smooth and spread on the cake. Not butter cream by a long shot—but fast!

Cookies

BROWNIES FROM CAKE MIX

With the horrendous price of chocolate, you'll get a less expensive brownie that is moist and delicious. With the appalling price of nuts, you might want to omit them.

1 cup chocolate cake mix
1 egg
1 tablespoon butter or
    margarine

1 cup chopped nuts

Blend all the ingredients well, then turn into a buttered 8 inch square pan. Bake at 350°F for 20 minutes.

 If your group likes their brownies iced, try this. As soon as the hot cake comes out of the oven, lay on top some chocolate covered mints. As they melt, spread into a delectable icing.

LEMON COOKIES

I cannot recall where this recipe came from, but it's fast and very good. You must not substitute other brands or it won't work.

1 package Duncan Hines lemon
    cake mix
1 egg

2½ cups Cool Whip
confectioners sugar

Mix together the cake mix, egg and Cool Whip.

Shape the dough into teaspoon size balls. Roll in powdered sugar and arrange on a buttered baking sheet leaving room for the cookies to spread. Bake at 350°F for 15 to 20 minutes.

TINY BUTTER COOKIES

These tiny, tender cookies will be money in the bank before Christmas. This normal-looking recipe made 180 delicious morsels. Use two baking sheets, make 30 on each sheet, and three bakings will do it. These would be fine for the day when you're asked to bring cookies to a giant tea party, too. I have made them with all margarine but somehow Tiny Margarine Cookies doesn't sound as good.

½ cup butter
½ cup Crisco or margarine
1½ cups confectioners sugar,
   sifted
¼ teaspoon salt
1 teaspoon vanilla

1 egg
2 cups flour
1 teaspoon baking soda
1 teaspoon cream of tartar

Cream butter and shortening. Add sifted powdered sugar gradually, and beat until light. Add salt, vanilla and the egg and beat thoroughly.

Sift remaining dry ingredients and add to the creamed mixture. Chill for 1 hour or so. Form into ½ inch balls, that's about the size of a marble. Arrange on cookie sheets then flatten with a fork dipped in sugar. You have to press one without sugar first to get started—then it's quick. Make the ridges deep or you'll lose them in the baking. Bake at 350°F for about 13 minutes. They should be blonde.

JOYCE'S MOCHA FROSTED DROPS

Excellent chocolate cookies with a sweet foil of coffee frosting.

½ cup shortening
2 squares unsweetened
   chocolate
1 cup brown sugar
1 egg
½ teaspoon vanilla
½ cup buttermilk (or sour milk)

1½ cups flour
½ teaspoon baking powder
½ teaspoon baking soda
¼ teaspoon salt
½ cup chopped walnuts
1 cup semi sweet chocolate bits

Melt the shortening and 2 squares of chocolate together. Cool for 10 minutes.

Stir in the brown sugar, then beat in the egg, vanilla and buttermilk. Sift the dry ingredients together and fold into the chocolate mixture. Stir in the nuts and chocolate bits.

Drop from a teaspoon onto greased cookie sheets and bake at 375°F for 10 minutes. Cool before frosting.

Mocha Frosting:

¼ cup butter
2 tablespoons cocoa
2 teaspoons instant powdered
   coffee
dash of salt

2½ cups confectioners sugar
1½ teaspoons vanilla
enough milk to make
   spreadable

Cream the butter, cocoa, coffee powder and salt. Beat in the sugar and vanilla, then add enough milk, a wee bit at a time, to make a smooth, spreadable icing.

MOLASSES COOKIES

Soft, spicy cookies that will disappear all too fast. These are family specials.

¾ cup margarine
1 cup brown sugar
1 egg
¼ cup molasses
2¼ cups sifted flour

2 teaspoons baking soda
¼ teaspoon salt
½ teaspoon powdered cloves
1 teaspoon cinnamon
1 teaspoon ginger

Thoroughly cream together the margarine, sugar, egg and molasses. Sift the sifted flour again with the soda, salt and spices. Stir into the molasses mixture to make a dough. Chill.

When chilled, roll into walnut-sized balls and dip just the tops in granulated sugar. Place on a greased cookie sheet 3 inches apart. Bake at 375°F for 10 to 12 minutes until just set, not hard.

ORANGE BLOSSOMS

More confection than cookie, these little balls would serve even as sweet little after dinner bites.

1 pound confectioners sugar,
    sifted
2 cans orange juice concentrate
    (6 ounce size)

2 sticks butter
2 packages vanilla wafers,
    crushed (12 ounce size)
grated coconut

Combine all ingredients except coconut thoroughly. Chill at least 1 hour. Form into small balls and roll in grated coconut. Keep refrigerated.

PEANUT BUTTER BALLS

At a picnic where these appeared, even the men asked for the recipe!

2 teaspoons soft butter
1 cup crunchy peanut butter
2 cups confectioners sugar
15 maraschino cherries, cut up

1 tablespoon cherry syrup
8 semi sweet chocolate squares,
   melted
2 cups chopped nuts

Mix everything except chocolate and nuts together. Roll into balls, dip in chocolate until coated, then roll in the finely chopped nuts.

IRENE'S SEVEN LAYER COOKIES

More candies than cookies, sister Irene's voluptuous, stratified sweets. Easy. Expensive.

1 stick margarine, melted in a
   9 x 9 x 2 inch pan
1 cup Graham cracker crumbs
1 cup coconut
1 small package chocolate bits

1 small package butterscotch
   bits
1 can condensed milk (15
   ounces)
1¼ cups chopped pecans

To the melted butter, add the crumbs. Make a bottom layer of crumbs, then layer all ingredients in the order listed, topping with pecans. Bake in a 350°F oven for 35 minutes. Cool well before cutting into small squares. Very small.

SWEDISH SPRITZ

How well I remember watching my Mother making these delicate butter cookies, hanging over the kitchen table, hoping to get a broken-off piece. They taste good even before they're baked! This is Connie Metcalf's grandmother's recipe, and it's a winner. You need a cookie press.

1 cup butter	2 to 2½ cups flour
⅔ cup sugar	1 teaspoon almond extract
3 egg yolks	

Cream the butter, then add sugar, egg yolks and almond extract, and beat thoroughly.

Add the flour very carefully. Too little, and the cookies won't hold their ridges. Too much, and they will be dry. Do not chill the dough or you'll have a hard time getting it through the press.

Shape the cookies with the press—my Mother made O's and S's with the small-toothed opening, and washboards with the wider one. If they need more flour, you can tell because the ridges will disappear.

Bake on cookie sheets at 375°F for 7 minutes. They should not be brown but blonde.

Join the Club

When you're sitting under the dryer, turning the pages of the latest glossy home and garden magazine, do you feel faint and ill with longing for those hangar-size, glamorous kitchens?

Do you positively ache for those miles of counter space? That range that obligingly charcoal grills, surrounds your roast or loaf with gentle currents of air, cleans itself and turns itself into a griddle when you choose?

Join the club.

Do you hanker after new small appliances, even though you know there isn't another square foot of space in your kitchen? Do you mail order gadgets that open oysters, knives that slice cheese differently, barbecue aprons with bon mots imprinted, and yet another recipe file?

You are a natural member.

You need to enroll in Kitchen Shops Anonymous, the organization for those of us who compulsively reach for everything that's new in cookware. (Your husband may be considered for membership, too, when on the first warm Spring day, he comes home with a charcoal grill that would do for a platoon.)

We are the klutzes who will shell out an astounding amount of hard cash for that specifically designed baking dish, that copper mold, that chic accessory—especially if it has Made in France on the bottom. It isn't always that we set out to make these purchases. We put ourselves in the shop, and let it happen.

The principal problem is that we don't replace, we add to.

Overcome with pangs of nostalgia when we attempt to replace the old Dutch oven, we have second thoughts. Then, up it goes on top of the shelves along with the oversized casserole we've used twice in three years. Or down it goes, to the basement shelf to sit alongside the tiny fryer, the ice cream maker, the Belgian waffle iron. Those we acquired during a seasonal madness we must learn to guard against.

I think of it as the Christmas scam. It begins around the middle of October every year. Then the small appliance manufacturers begin to tease us, in living color, with some device that seems more desirable every week. Worse, even though we remain strong, our husbands ultimately see this as the perfect Christmas gift. No shopping.

Where are they now, these gifts of yesteryear?

You know.

Pie in the Sky...

Fruits, Nuts and Others

Written down recipes for pies appear extraordinarily early in English lore. From 1378, a recipe for a Brie Tart is for all the world like today's quiche.

Bake it in a trap, the recipe advises, the trap being the crust. Another interesting word for the shell was coffin, which comes up in another recipe for a cheese pie.

Many of the pies of the early centuries were filled with meat or cheese rather than fruits or sweets. One reason for their popularity was that, in the absence of forks, food was easier to eat in a crust.

I have found one ancient recipe for a honey and saffron quiche, reputedly served at the coronation of Henry IV in October of 1399, and the first one I know of for apple tart is in a collection dated 1381.

Today, when we ask for a piece of pie, we mean a dessert pie, hopefully with a flaky crust and a flavorful filling. Making the crust is child's play, and if you have a food processor, fast as lightning. If you don't have, as they used to say, a light hand for pastry, by all means use the good mixes. Fool proof.

Many of our pies have a rather symbolic nature, like a cherry pie for Washington's birthday, pumpkin pie for Thanksgiving, and mince for Christmas. Apple pie is consonant with being an American. Huckleberry pie somehow connotes an earlier innocence.

In addition to the heavy rich pies of winter, we now enjoy the cold chiffons and the easy freezer pies. Almost everybody likes pie, and especially when it's *à la mode* with ice cream.

If you haven't branched out in the crust department, you might look up pâté brisée in a general cookbook. It is a shorter, flakier crust which is very good. And for tarts, dessert tarts, look into pâté brisée sucrée, which is simply the same crust but with sugar added to the flour at the outset.

Keeping the crust in shape when you pre-bake can be accomplished by piercing rows of holes with a fork before baking. If you want to keep the crust absolutely flat, fill it with dried beans while it bakes. Some recipes suggest foil, then the beans, but this makes it damp and slightly soggy I find.

If your crust is going to be filled with a very wet filling, bake it slightly first, then add the filling. Or, as in the Strawberry Pie which follows, spread it with softened cream cheese which makes a protective layer. We're talking about avoiding that damp, quarter inch layer that you encounter so frequently in store pies.

When you make your own crust, you always have some left. Don't throw it out, use it. You can make some handsome little leaves, fasten them to the top crust with a bit of egg white, and dress up your pie.

When the children were small, I used to roll out the leftovers, cut into squares, sprinkle with cinnamon and sugar and make little treats.

Some of the most handsome pies in the whole world are the European tarts, fruit filled, arranged in striking patterns, and glazed with melted jams, or sugared and browned into caramel glaze under the broiler. These are great fun to experiment with. They do not necessarily have to be made of one fruit; you can make a stunning tart with, say, peaches, apricots and plums arranged in a pretty design. Custard often lurks below.

I have tried to find some unusual and good pies for you, assuming that you already have a lemon meringue and apple recipe you wouldn't change for the world. Among them, maybe you'll find your pie in the sky.

CHOCOLATE MINT PIES

Three at a blow! A wonderful recipe from one of those old fashioned home style restaurants, fast disappearing from our lives. This pie freezes very well—so make one to please and two to freeze.

Crust:

1 box graham crackers (1 pound)   2½ sticks butter or margarine

Do not melt the butter. Soften it at room temperature, then cut into, or mix with the crackers that have been rolled out very fine or processed.

Press the mixture into 3 pie pans, 9 inch. Bake at 250°F until firm but not brown. Cool before filling.

Chocolate Filling:

**1 pound butter or margarine,
    softened
2 boxes confectioners sugar
8 large eggs
2 boxes Hershey's bitter
    chocolate, melted**

**3 teaspoons pure mint or
    peppermint extract**

Melt the chocolate over boiling water while you cream the soft butter with the powdered sugar. Wise to mix a little by hand first or your mixer will throw a film of XXX all over the kitchen.

Add the eggs, one at a time, beating after each addition. Add the melted chocolate and finally the mint extract, mixing well.

Divide the filling among the 3 pie shells. It will be very thick and set up even more when refrigerated. Serve with a small scoop of vanilla ice cream on top.

COCONUT CHOCOLATE SILK PIE

My doorman buzzed me one day to announce I had a package. To my delight it was a section of this pie, made by a friend with the obvious injunction, "Eat me." I did. Here it is, sinfully rich, deliciously self serving.

To make the pie shell, butter a pie plate lavishly with margarine. Press shredded coconut onto it until the whole surface is coated with a thick layer. Bake at 300°F until golden.

Filling:

2 ounces bitter chocolate	2 tablespoons instant coffee
1 cup margarine	1 cup coarsely chopped nuts
1 cup sugar	(pecans, walnuts)
2 eggs	rum or brandy

Melt the chocolate and allow it to cool slightly. Cream the margarine with the sugar in your electric mixer. Add the eggs, 1 at a time as you continue to beat, 3 minutes per egg. Add the cooled chocolate, coffee, nuts and a dollop of brandy or rum to taste. Turn into the coconut shell and chill well before serving.

CRANBERRY-RAISIN PIE

This would be a nice change for a holiday dinner.

1 unbaked pie shell	1 cup sugar
pastry for lattice top	2 heaping tablespoons flour
1½ cups fresh cranberries,	½ cup water
coarsely ground	1 teaspoon vanilla
1 cup raisins, coarsely ground	

The fruit should be ground or chopped coarsely through a grinder or very quickly in the processor.

Mix all remaining ingredients with the fruit and turn into the unbaked pie shell. Cut strips and lattice the top. Bake at 450°F for 10 minutes, then reduce heat to 350°F for 25 or 30 minutes longer. Serve topped with vanilla ice cream or whipped cream.

SELF-FROSTING LEMON PIE

This old fashioned recipe came to me from Nebraska, but I have since learned the same sort of recipe is used around Lancaster, Pennsylvania where it is called Montgomery Pie.

1 large lemon, pulp, juice and grated rind	3 tablespoons flour
1 cup sugar	¾ cup milk
2 egg yolks, well beaten	butter, the size of a walnut, melted
2 egg whites, well beaten	unbaked pie shell

Stir together the lemon pulp, juice and rind with the sugar, egg yolks, flour and milk. Add the melted butter, then fold in the beaten egg whites gently.

Pour into an unbaked pie shell and bake at 350°F for about 40 minutes.

 As the pie bakes, the filling turns into a sort of pudding with a spongy cake topping.

PECAN CUSTARD PIE

This recipe came from a handwritten book dated 1869 by a home-steader's wife in the midwest.

1 baked pie shell

Filling:

3 egg yolks, slightly beaten
½ cup sugar
¼ teaspoon salt
1 cup milk
1 tablespoon unflavored gelatin

¼ cup ice water
3 egg whites, stiffly beaten
1 teaspoon vanilla
½ cup pecans, coarsely chopped

Separate eggs. Cook slightly beaten yolks, sugar, salt and milk together over hot water in the top of your double boiler until the custard thickens.

In a small bowl, sprinkle the gelatin over the ice water and let it dissolve. Add to the hot custard, stirring until it disappears. Cool the custard.

Beat the egg whites stiff. When the custard mixture begins to set, fold in the egg whites, vanilla and chopped nuts. Turn into the pie shell and chill. Garnish with whipped cream and/or a sprinkle of finely chopped nuts.

PISTACHIO WREATH PIE

A festive dessert especially nice at Christmas time when you can decorate the whipped cream wreath with candied red cherries and green citron, holiday colors.

1½ cups coconut cookies, crumbled
1 tablespoon Amaretto liqueur
¼ cup melted butter
2 packages pistachio instant pudding (3⅝ ounce size)
3 cups Half and Half

⅓ cup Amaretto liqueur
1 can crushed pineapple, well drained (20 ounces)
1 cup heavy cream
2 tablespoons confectioners sugar
garnishes

Mix the crumbs, the tablespoon of amaretto, and the butter in a bowl. Press the mixture into a 9 inch pie pan to form a crust.

Combine pudding and Half and Half in another bowl, mixing until smooth, then adding the ⅓ cup of Amaretto. Fold in the drained pineapple and turn the filling into the pie shell, swirling the top. Chill until set.

When ready to serve, whip the cream with sugar and spoon it around the pie edge like a wreath. Garnish and serve.

AUNT EVELYN'S PUMPKIN CHIFFON PIE

1 envelope unflavored gelatin
¾ cup brown sugar
½ teaspoon salt
½ teaspoon nutmeg
1 teaspoon cinnamon
¾ cup skim milk

3 eggs, separated
1½ cups canned puréed pumpkin
¼ cup sugar
whipped cream
1 baked pie shell, 9 inch size

In the top of a double boiler, combine gelatin, brown sugar, salt, nutmeg, and cinnamon. Stir in milk, egg yolks and pumpkin and mix well until smooth.

Cook over gently boiling water until the gelatin is dissolved and the mixture is heated through, about 15 minutes. Remove from heat and chill until thickened.

Beat the egg whites until they hold stiff peaks, then beat in ¼ cup sugar. Fold whites into the pumpkin mixture and turn into the pie shell. Chill. Top with sweetened whipped cream. Serves eight.

RUM PIE WITH BLUEBERRIES

An excellent dessert and a chance to correct a historical wrong. When we write graham cracker without the upper case, we do a great disservice to Dr. Graham, one of the first advocates of health foods and the deviser of whole wheat bread and graham, no, Graham crackers.

1 ¼ cups Graham cracker crumbs
¼ cup soft butter or margarine
2 tablespoons sugar
4 packages cream cheese (3 ounce size)

½ cup sugar
2 eggs, well beaten
¼ teaspoon rum extract
2 cups fresh blueberries, washed and dried

Topping:

1 cup sour cream
2 tablespoons sugar

2 tablespoons sweet sherry

Make a crust of the Graham crackers, butter and sugar, mixing them well and pressing into an ungreased 9 inch pie pan.

In the mixer bowl, beat the cream cheese until it is fluffy, then gradually beat in the sugar. Add the eggs, beat well, then add the rum extract. Taste. You might want more rum flavoring.

Fold in the blueberries and turn the mixture into the crumb crust. Bake at 375°F for 25 minutes or until the filling has set. Remove and cool.

Simply stir together the topping ingredients and spread over the pie, swirling if you feel creative. Garnish with plump blueberries, chill and serve.

 An easy way to sort and dry the berries at the same time is to wash them, then put at the far end of a length of paper towel. As you stem and discard, roll the perfect berries toward you. They dry as they roll.

RUM NUT APPLE PIE

Favorite recipe of my food page editor, Margaret Crabtree.

pastry for a 2-crust pie

6 cups apples, peeled, sliced thin	**1 tablespoon milk**
¼ cup chopped walnuts	**1 tablespoon rum flavoring**
1 cup granulated sugar	**¼ teaspoon nutmeg**
2 tablespoons flour	**¼ teaspoon cinnamon**

Mix all ingredients together in a large bowl and turn into an unbaked 9 inch pie shell, dot with butter and cover with unbaked top crust.

Bake at 425°F for 15 minutes, then reduce heat and bake at 350°F for 45 minutes more. When the pie comes hot out of the oven, brush on topping with a pastry brush. The pie will look white and glazed. Serves eight.

Topping:

½ cup confectioners sugar	**3 tablespoons butter**
2 tablespoons rum	**1 teaspoon milk**

Cream together until smooth and spreadable.

STRAWBERRY PIE

When I still had a ravenous family around me, this was one of the four-star desserts at our table.

1 unbaked pie shell, 9 inch

Prick all over with a fork and bake to a crisp and lightly golden color.

Filling:

1 package softened cream cheese
a little cream or milk
1 quart strawberries

¼ to ½ cup sugar depending on berries' sweetness
2 tablespoons cornstarch
whipped cream for topping

Soften the softened cream cheese with a little milk until it is easily spreadable. Carefully smooth it over the bottom of the pie shell.

Clean and stem the berries. Cut the extra large in half. Arrange about a quarter of the berries on the cream cheese. Slice the remaining berries and toss them with the sugar in a saucepan until the juices develop. Use some of the juice to dissolve the cornstarch.

Now cook the strawberries with the cornstarch added until the mixture thickens and clears. Cool, then pour into the shell and refrigerate. Serve topped with whipped cream. Serves eight.

Contentious Cooks

Food writers go through life happily certain that somewhere out there are millions of women standing at millions of ranges, happily stirring and baking, sniffing and tasting, presiding over tables that look like covers from Better Homes and Gardens.

Actually, a lot of women don't like to cook, and that's a fact.

Questions laid on the anti-cooking crowd provide answers of some diversity.

From an intellectual: "Culturally, females are conditioned to please men with food. Your man should want more than that."

From a slick chick: "When I was cooking really well I got FAT!"

From a highly creative, highly disorganized female: "Every time I think I have it all together, I'm out of something—a lemon, tomato paste, whatever."

From a busy young mother: "Dinner comes at the end of the day when I'm tired, really tired. Cooking is the last thing I want to do after a full day of babies."

To the last plaint, I addressed the possibility of a crockpot started in the morning. She looked at me with her big blue eyes and said, "I don't like to handle things like meat and onions in the morning." Visible shudder.

From a good cook weary of it all: "My husband thinks nothing of taking long telephone calls at the middle of dinner, and never, never notices the special efforts I make."

Well, if you fall into any of these categories, there are steps to be taken, props for support, pleasures to be had.

Inevitability. Inevitability connotes sameness. Recommended is the theatrical approach. Dazzle yourself with new dishes. Have a picnic on the living room floor in the middle of winter. Just for the hell of it, get paper hats and celebrate Mozart's birthday. Have a buffet en famille. Make every dinner an event. And for your own personal prop, insist on dinner out one night aweek, even if it's only a Big Mac.

Getting fat. There are at least ten excellent cookbooks on the market full of recipes for low fat cooking. Anyhow, dearie, just because you gain weight, don't punish your calorie burning kids and your husband who expect the solace and comfort of good food.

Out of it. Do you realize that many classical recipes were created because someone was out of something. Poulet Marengo, for one, was improvised on a battlefield by Napoleon's chef in such an emergency. Creativity flourishes in the kitchen. Learn how to put this in place of that and you may wind up with a cookbook of your own.

Tired mamma. Not hers the luxury of choice as to how she will spend her time. My recommendation is to use every shortcut in the book. Try to balance meals that taste OK, and don't try to shoot for the stars. With a little help from Himself, you can still swim out of that sea of Gerber's.

Pleasing men. Why not please both of you, not just him? Good dining is the second best shared experience between men and women. Get him in on the plot. Then you can each cook to please the other, and knock off the analysis.

Afraid. Only one way to go. Charge! Lay down Fear of Flying, get a firm hold on yourself and enjoy the Ecstasy of Cooking—go at it, one dish at a time.

Indifference. If your husband comes home with a pocketful of indifference, maybe a few indifferent meals are in order. Put out a frozen dinner he can heat up, and you go out to the flicks. He'll notice, he'll notice.

But the best way to stir your own interest in food is to read. Read cookbooks and great food writers like Joseph Wechsberg and M. F. K. Fisher. The public library has hundreds of volumes waiting for you. I guarantee that you will slowly stir toward the kitchen with a revitalized interest in the one fine art we are all privileged to practice.

A Sweet Afterthought

Getting Your Just Desserts

The line that's been floating around lately, "You can't be too thin or too rich," has done its share in what seems to be a general stamping out of desserts.

But it falls on the deaf ears of a lot of people who only go through the entrée to get to the dessert. For them, the high point is the sweet finale, and if they don't get a dessert, they feel cheated.

Perhaps you have switched to fruit and cheese, or even to low-cal substitutes. I personally think the way to go is to cut down, not cut out, to reduce the size of servings. Tiny tarts, thin slices of cake, a few good cookies are all fine ways to end a meal.

But when you want to serve a festive dessert, do make it a pretty one. Remember when restaurants used to bring a dessert trolley to your table? The sight of voluptuous chocolate, clouds of whipped cream, and exotic glazed tortes would turn strong men faint, and turn dieting women into uncaring calorie consumers.

Nobody goes ooh, ah, at the sight of a stew, however good it is. But bring on a mold with ribbons of whipped cream and beautiful garnishes, and you're a sudden star. God knows, most of us get little enough attention, so if this is your thing, go to it!

Beautiful desserts can be time consuming and difficult, or they can be a breeze. Today, I believe most women want to make a pretty dessert, but not spend the whole day on it.

If you don't have time to make a cheesecake, buy a plain one, then cover the top with berries or fruit and glaze with melted jelly. You'll get applause.

Buy a sponge cake, slice it horizontally, soak it with rum and fill with ricotta or custard. Top with whipped cream.

Anything in a mold is lovely to look at, even if it's only a fruit gelatin.

All sorts of puddings, box or home made, taste better in a pretty dish with a garnish. If it's a bread or rice pudding, be free with the raisins. If it's a brown betty or similar, serve an English custard alongside, that's a spoonable custard. By the way, that custard, well chilled, tastes marvelous over fresh strawberries or blueberries.

Tiny dessert tarts give people the option of eating one, just a sweet afterthought. Little cream puffs, miniature French pastries are admirable for that one rich bite.

But ahead of you lies a tender trap, to be avoided if you're counting the high cost of calories.

BAKED STUFFED APPLES

An all American favorite laced with an all Italian liqueur.

½ cup apricot preserves
½ cup amaretto liqueur
2 cups chopped almonds

1 cup golden raisins
8 large, tart baking apples, cored

Melt the preserves in a small sauce pan, and stir in the amaretto. Put half the mixture in a bowl and add to it the almonds and raisins. Divide this stuffing among the cored apples, wrap each apple in foil, and set in a pan with 1 inch or so of water.

Bake at 350°F for 45 minutes. Remove from the oven, take off the foil and empty out any remaining water from the pan. Brush the apples with the reserved glaze and return them to the oven for 5 minutes until they are lovely and shiny. Serve with cold sweet or sour cream.

BANANAS FOSTER with ICE CREAM

You can increase this recipe and serve as is without ice cream, but here we use this famous recipe as a topping.

2 bananas, peeled, sliced crosswise	2 shakes of cinnamon
4 tablespoons brown sugar	½ cup chopped walnuts
4 tablespoons melted butter	2 tablespoons dark rum
	1 pint butter crunch ice cream

In a medium skillet, melt the butter, stir in the brown sugar, cinnamon and the walnuts. Add the bananas and cook about 3 minutes. Heat the rum and pour over, ignite, and let blaze while you gently shake the pan to keep everything from sticking.

Put the ice cream in 4 dessert dishes or stemmed glasses, and spoon the bananas over the top. Serves four.

BLUEBERRY CHEESE CAKE

This is a very pretty dessert with the big blueberries glazed handsomely. It will make people very happy.

1 cup Graham cracker crumbs
2 tablespoons sugar
¼ cup melted butter
2 packages cream cheese, softened (8 ounce size)
1 cup sour cream
¾ cup sugar

1 teaspoon vanilla
2 tablespoons flour
4 eggs
2 cups fine blueberries, washed and dried
⅓ cup blueberry jelly

Mix the crumbs, sugar and butter together to make a crust mixture. Pat into the bottom of a 9 inch spring form pan.

Cream the cream cheese until soft, then gradually beat into it the sour cream, sugar, flour and vanilla. Beat in the eggs, 1 at a time. Pour the mixture over the crumb crust and bake at 325°F for 1 hour or more until it tests done.

Remove from the oven and cool. Carefully now, run a knife around the edges to loosen. Unspring from the pan. Cool.

In a small saucepan, heat the jelly until it melts. Use a bit of this glaze to paint the top of the cake. It is sticky and will hold the blueberries on while you arrange them all over the top. Finish by drizzling the melted jelly all over the berries. Chill and serve. Serves eight.

OLD FASHIONED BREAD PUDDING

⅓ cup raisins
4 slices white bread
1 stick butter, melted
2 eggs

⅔ cup sugar
2 cups milk
1 teaspoon vanilla

Strew the raisins in the bottom of a 1 quart casserole which you have buttered generously. Cut the bread into wide strips and dip both sides of each piece in the melted butter. Arrange the bread over the raisins in the dish.

Beat the eggs with the sugar, add milk and vanilla, and pour the mixture over the bread. Set in a pan of hot water and bake for 50 minutes at 375°F. Serves six.

CHOCOLATE POTS DE CRÈME

These are usually made on top of the stove but here they go in the oven. Very small servings are indicated because of the deep richness of this dessert. It comes out rather like the chocolate filling in very expensive Swiss chocolates.

1 cup Half and Half	¼ cup sugar
2 ounces semi sweet chocolate	pinch of salt
1 ounce bitter chocolate	1½ teaspoons vanilla
3 egg yolks	

Heat the Half and Half and melt the chocolate in the hot cream.

Beat the egg yolks with the sugar and salt using a hand whisk. Gradually add the chocolate mixture to the egg mixture, whisking gently. Add vanilla, then strain the mixture into a measuring cup which will make it easy to pour.

Fill 6 pots de crème, and put on the lids. Set them in a pan with 1 inch of hot water and bake at 350°F for 30 minutes. Chill and serve.

CRÈME BRÛLÉE

Unforgettably rich and creamy, this famous dessert is not difficult to make, it just takes a little care. When finished you will have rich custard topped with thin, brittle caramel.

3 cups heavy cream
6 tablespoons granulated sugar
6 egg yolks

2 teaspoons vanilla
½ cup fine light brown sugar

Heat the cream in the top of a double boiler over simmering water. Stir in the white sugar until it dissolves.

Beat the egg yolks vigorously until they are light and pale colored. Pour the hot cream very gradually into the egg yolks, stirring with a will. Add vanilla. When all mixed, turn into a baking dish set in a pan with water 1 inch deep. Use a wide baking dish. You want a lot of the topping.

Bake the custard in a 300°F oven for 35 minutes until set. A knife inserted in the center should come out clean.

Chill the custard thoroughly. When ready to finish, sprinkle the top absolutely evenly with the brown sugar. If it's lumpy, sift it. If there are any high places when it goes under the broiler they will brown too quickly.

Now, run the custard under the broiler, and do not take your eyes off it. The minute the sugar melts and glazes, remove and chill until serving time.

Offer very small servings. It is extremely rich and will do for eight.

I have done this too early and had the glaze soften. Don't be upset. It still tastes wonderful. But when the glaze is crisp as brittle, it's very showoff to crack it with the back of a spoon in order to serve.

RITA TUTTLE'S TINY CHEESE CAKES

3 packages cream cheese
   (8 ounce size)
⅔ cup sugar
3 large eggs

1 teaspoon vanilla
vanilla wafers
fruit topping

Soften the cream cheese, add sugar, eggs and vanilla. Beat well with your electric mixer. Put one vanilla wafer at the bottom of each of 10 individual foil cupcake cups, then fill ¾ full with the cheese mixture. Bake on a cookie sheet at 350°F for 15 minutes. Cool and consume, or foil wrap and freeze.

When ready to serve, remove from the freezer at least 30 minutes ahead, turn each cake out on a dessert plate, and top with cherry or blueberry pie filling mix, or fresh fruit of your choice.

CRÊPES GRAND MARNIER

I know a young woman who makes crêpes frequently and doesn't own a crêpe pan. She took a few minutes one day to scout the kitchen and measure the batter, and she discovered a ladle that holds exactly the amount she requires for a proper crêpe. Now all her crêpes are alike—in a plain old skillet.

Crêpes:

⅞ cup flour
¼ cup sugar
3 eggs
2 tablespoons Grand Marnier
    liqueur

¼ teaspoon vanilla
dash of salt
2 tablespoons melted butter
1½ cups milk

Sift flour and sugar together. Beat in the eggs, 1 at a time, then add Grand Marnier, vanilla and salt. Stir in the butter and the milk.

Cook the crêpes, 1 at a time, in a well buttered 6 inch skillet or crêpe pan over fairly high flame. Brown both sides lightly, and fold the finished crêpes. Arrange on a chafing dish or on individual dessert plates.

The Sauce:

3 tablespoons butter
3 tablespoons sugar
3 tablespoons water

¼ cup Grand Marnier
1 teaspoon grated orange
    peel

Melt the butter and dissolve the sugar in it in a small saucepan. Add water, Grand Marnier and orange peel. Stir well and heat for just a few minutes. Pour over crêpes and serve. Serves six.

 If you like, you can heat some liqueur and blaze the crêpes after adding the sauce. But they're really delicious without being flamed.

GLORIA'S FLAN

A superb caramel custard made in an unusual way. This big recipe will serve twelve for a dinner party but you can cut it in half using four eggs and cooking just half as long.

¼ cup sugar
7 eggs
1½ cups sugar
2 cans undiluted evaporated
    milk

1 teaspoon vanilla
1 tablespoon grated lemon or
    lime rind

In the top pan of a double boiler, on the fire, caramelize the ¼ cup sugar this way: Boil sugar with a tablespoon of water until the sugar caramelizes. Immediately tilt in all directions to coat the bottom and lower sides of the pan evenly. Set aside.

In a large bowl, beat the eggs with a whisk, adding the 1½ cups of sugar gradually. Whisk in the vanilla and grated rind, and finally all of the milk.

Bring about 1 inch of water to a boil in the bottom of the boiler. Pour the custard mix into the caramelized top, set it over the bottom and cook with the lid on for 90 minutes. Check the water level from time to time, keeping it at about 1 inch. When you check, remove the lid as well and wipe away the water that will accumulate.

When the flan is firm, test by inserting a thin knife into the center. When it comes out clean, the custard is done. Remove from the bottom pan and let cool to room temperature, uncovered. Serve at room temperature or chill in the refrigerator.

To unmold, carefully loosen the top edges, put a serving plate over, then overturn. The caramel will run down the sides making a beautiful dessert to present. Serves twelve.

COGNAC MOUSSE

What could be nicer after dinner than a taste of cognac? Word of caution: When you make frozen desserts be sure to remove them from the freezer in time to make them edible. Nothing beats trying to spoon up a gelid solid. The time will depend on the size and even the shape of your dessert dish. For this, use the best bakery macaroons (or home made).

8 macaroons, crumbled
½ cup brandy
¼ cup cream

½ cup sugar
1 pint whipping cream

Mix together the macaroons, brandy, cream and sugar. Let mellow until well flavored all through. Whip the pint of cream until thick enough to hold a point, then fold the macaroon mixture into it. Spoon into dessert dishes and freeze. Makes six to eight servings.

 I just thought of a pretty dessert garnish I used to make and how well it would go with this. Pick a lot of 1½ to 2 inch rose leaves from your yard. Try to find some that have heavy veining on the back. Wash and dry them. Melt chocolate, semi sweet or milk, lay the leaves out, vein side up, and with a small spatula, cover them with melted chocolate tidily. Chill well, then remove the leaf and you'll have pretty chocolate leaves to perk up the top of a dessert or cake.

G.A.'S MANDARIN ORANGES

Allowing a half can of mandarin orange slices per person, drain the fruit and really chill it. Heat a generous amount of good orange marmalade just enough to warm it into a softer state.

When ready to serve, put the chilled fruit in dessert dishes, glaze the top liberally with the marmalade, then crown with a good dollop of sour cream.

PEARS PORCUPINE

Very easy to make and pretty.

3 large fresh pears, poached, or,
   1 can large pear halves,
   drained
1 envelope whole blanched
   almonds

½ cup melted currant jelly
1 tablespoon crème de cassis
   liqueur
strawberry ice cream

Toast the almonds in a slow oven until golden. Poach the pear halves in a light sugar syrup or, easier used big halves canned. Stud the pears with almonds à la porcupine. Chill.

When ready to serve, melt the jelly with the liqueur. Lay each pear on a serving of ice cream then mask the pear with the red jelly. Serves six.

TINY PECAN TARTS

These little tarts freeze splendidly and can be used for a small dessert, or may show up at a coffee or tea party.

8 ounces cream cheese, softened
1 cup butter or margarine,
    softened
2 cups flour
2 eggs, slightly beaten

1½ cups light brown sugar
1½ teaspoons vanilla
pinch of salt
2 cups chopped pecans

In the blender, processor or by hand, blend together the cheese and butter. Stir in flour, or add to processor and make a pastry dough.

Divide into 48 little balls if you have 4 tiny tart pans, 12 tarts each. Press each ball in a hole and form a shell. Don't try to bring the edges up—just make a smooth edge. If you have only 1 pan, make 12, and put the rest of the dough in the refrigerator to make after the first batch comes out.

In a bowl, combine the eggs, sugar, vanilla and salt, then fold in the nuts. Spoon the mixture into the shells and bake 25 to 30 minutes in a 325°F oven until set.

 This same kind of shell can be used in making very good appetizers. See Baby Quiche in the index.

FRESH PINEAPPLE, FRAMBOISE CREAM

Framboise is a raspberry flavored liqueur. Delectable.

2 fresh, ripe pineapples
2 tablespoons sugar

2 tablespoons Framboise

Peel, core and de-eye the pineapples, and cut the meat into 1 inch cubes. Sprinkle with the sugar and Framboise and chill thoroughly.

The Cream:

4 egg yolks
½ cup sugar plus 2 tablespoons
1 cup Framboise

1 cup warm milk
1 teaspoon vanilla
½ cup heavy cream

In a double boiler top, combine sugar and egg yolks, beating until they are pale and smooth. Add the warm milk and set the pan over boiling water. Cook until the sauce thickens enough to heavily coat a metal spoon.

Pour the sauce into a cold bowl, add the liqueur and vanilla and chill. Whip the cream. Fold in. Keep in the refrigerator until serving time, then spoon into the custard any pineapple juice that has accumulated in the pineapple bowl. Place the pineapple in dessert dishes, and serve the sauce separately. Serves eight.

PRALINE ICE CREAM BALLS

12 Heath candy bars
ice cream—vanilla, coffee or
    chocolate

Chill the Heath bars. Put a few at a time between wax paper, and whack them or roll them into chocolaty praline. Using an ice cream scoop make balls, one at a time. Roll them totally in the praline and freeze immediately.

Take them out a few minutes before serving. If you want a voluptuous experience, have some chocolate sauce on the side.

PUMPKIN BOMBE WITH MINCEMEAT SAUCE

2 cups canned pumpkin purèe	½ teaspoon nutmeg
1 cup brown sugar, firmly packed	¼ teaspoon salt
	¼ teaspoon ground cloves
2 teaspoons cinnamon	2 quarts vanilla ice cream

In the large bowl of your electric mixer, blend pumpkin, spices, sugar and salt. Chop the ice cream into chunks and, with the electric mixer on low speed, beat the ice cream into the pumpkin mixture. Beat until smooth.

Pour the mixture into a 10 to 12 cup mold, forcing a spatula down to break up the bubbles. Freeze for twenty four hours. Unmold on a chilled plate and return to the freezer. When hardened again, wrap in plastic film and store in the freezer.

Flaming Mincemeat Sauce:

1 jar mincemeat (1 pound, 12 ounces)	grated rind of 1 orange
	¼ cup brandy

When ready to serve the bombe: Combine mincemeat and orange rind in a chafing dish until bubbly. Warm brandy, then ignite and pour, flaming, over the mincemeat. Keep the sauce warm over a very low flame until you serve.

Place the bombe on your prettiest serving plate, pour the hot mincemeat over and serve.

 If you don't have a chafing dish or don't want to bother with it, flame the mincemeat and keep it hot over water in the top of the double boiler.

WELLWOOD CLUB RICE

The Wellwood Club is a boating club in Maryland. The original old frame building which was visited by the first President Roosevelt and other notables has practically fallen apart. But the new one still serves the notable rice pudding.

2 quarts milk	1 cup sugar
1 orange, juice and grated rind	1 tablespoon vanilla extract
1 cup rice	2 eggs

Bring the milk to a full boil. Put in the rice and ½ cup of the sugar, the rind and the juice of the orange. Simmer, covered, for 1 hour. With a wire whisk, beat the remaining ingredients in a bowl. Stir into the cooked rice. Put in a serving bowl and sprinkle with mixed sugar and cinnamon, chilled. Serves six.

RUM PUDDING

Five minutes from start to finish—that's a fast dessert, and it's from scratch.

2 eggs	2 tablespoons strong coffee
1 small package chocolate bits (6 ounces)	¾ cup milk scalded
	2 tablespoons dark rum

Put all ingredients into your blender and buzz until smooth. Pour into individual serving dishes and top with a dollop of whipped cream when thoroughly chilled. Serves four.

STRAWBERRY TART

Here's a delicious beauty to make when the big juicy berries are plentiful.

1 tart shell (10 inch) baked

Filling:

⅓ cup flour
¾ cup sugar
pinch of salt
2 whole eggs
2 egg yolks

2 cups milk
4 good macaroons
1 tablespoon fraises du bois
   (strawberry liqueur)
2 tablespoons butter

Put the flour, sugar and salt in the top of your double boiler, not over hot water yet. Add 1 egg and 1 egg yolk and whisk in, then add the other egg and yolk and whisk more. In a saucepan, scald the milk and add it slowly to the egg mixture, stirring all the time.

Have the water hot in the bottom of the double boiler. Set the top over it and cook, whisking, stirring until the mixture thickens. Remove from heat and add the crumbled macaroons and the liqueur. While still warm, stir in the butter, then fill the tart shell and cool.

Topping:

as many beautiful washed, well
   dried strawberries as you
   like

Glaze:

½ cup currant jelly
1 tablespoon creme de cassis
   liqueur

Melt together and spoon or brush over the berries. It will be beautiful. Serves eight.

HUGUENOT TORTE

A traditional recipe from the Carolinas often used by a Charleston friend for big party dessert. It will serve sixteen but you can readily halve it for the family.

4 eggs
3 cups sugar
8 tablespoons flour
5 teaspoons baking powder
½ teaspoon salt

2 cups chopped tart cooking
    apples (peeled, cored)
2 cups chopped pecans or
    walnuts
2 teaspoons vanilla

In the big mixer bowl, beat the eggs until frothy and light and lemon colored. Beat in the sugar, flour, baking powder and salt just until smooth.

Fold in apples and nuts, stir in vanilla, and turn the batter into 2 well buttered pans, each 8 x 12 inches. Bake at 325°F about 45 minutes until crusty and browned. To serve, scoop up with a pancake turner, crusty part up, pile on a plate and slather with whipped cream.

If you prefer, cut into 16 pieces and top with whipped cream.

ITALIAN TRIFLE

Absolutely everything out of a box or bottle—but delectable and inexpensive, very easy to make.

1 package Italian small sponge cakes
1 package vanilla pudding mix
1 package chocolate pudding mix

milk for the puddings
rum
½ cup whipping cream

Make the puddings according to package directions—if you're in a big rush make the instant kind.

When the puddings are set proceed as follows: Cut each sponge in half horizontally and arrange 1 layer in the bottom of an 8 inch square pan or dish. Using a tablespoon, moisten each piece with as much rum as you like.

Over that, spoon the vanilla pudding. Make another layer of sponge, soak with rum, spoon over the chocolate pudding. Finish with a layer of sponge, pour on the rum and top with whipped cream. Serves eight.

FROZEN VANILLA SOUFFLÉ

The day I planned to try this next recipe was in the fall. Invited to a political coffee meeting, I lucked in. The hostess served her own home made perfect macaroons. Slipping two in my bag, I larcenously made my way home to the testing ground. Please, don't use supermarket macaroons. Get the best bakery ones you can—or make some.

1 pint vanilla ice cream,
    softened
2 crumbled macaroons
4 tablespoons Grand Marnier
½ cup heavy cream, whipped

2 tablespoons chopped toasted
    almonds
2 tablespoons confectioners
    sugar

Quickly, lightly mix the first 4 ingredients. Pour into a small mold and sprinkle the almonds and sugar over the top. Freeze. Serves four.

Sauce:

1 pint fresh strawberries or
    10 ounces frozen straw-
    berries

sugar to taste
4 tablespoons Grand Marnier

Heat sauce ingredients together. Serve warm over the icy soufflé.

My Gentlemen Callers

You wouldn't believe the number of men there are in my life.

They ring-up of an evening to share their problems with me, and our conversations are animated, frequently very long.

Like George Bernard Shaw and Ellen Terry, we never meet. We just communicate about our mutual pleasures and sometimes dillemmas, not in the theater, but in cookery.

These gentlemen callers cook. They are readers of my food page and ardent in their pursuit of good food. Ever increasing in numbers, they call for all sorts of reasons.

Sometimes they've lost a recipe. "I'm cooking for guests on Wednesday and can't find my Spaghetti Ferrara recipe." I give it to him over the phone.

Sometimes it's a what-do-I-do-now call. The man is halfway through a recipe, and startled by some development.

Sometimes it's chiding. "Where did you get the juice to thicken from the bourbon pork roast?" He had made it without covering and the volatile booze disappeared.

Where the man of the house used to be the barbecue specialist or the super salad maker, he now ventures into the wider world of the entreé in the kitchen.

But the reason this book is devoted to women is because men, except in rare cases, are not day-in, day-out cooks. They are weekend cooks, hobbyists, and would probably be somewhat put out if expected to get the kids' breakfasts or pack lunches. Exception—single parent homes where men have capably taken over.

Nevertheless, they are great fun to talk to, and I wouldn't miss a call. Sometimes they call just to tell me how well something turned out. Occasionally they'll give me a new recipe, or ask me to dig up a formula for making something they had in a restaurant.

One young bachelor I know can whip up a meal in nothing flat. He uses a wok and a microwave oven. Another caller is primarily a bread baker. Another makes his own sauerkraut, and looks constantly for the perfect scrapple.

It's a pleasure for me to watch this new freedom in men. I well remember the day when American men would have been terribly put out, and even threatened, if expected to assume a role in the kitchen.

Today, many new homes are built, or old ones remodeled to make a place for two cooks. Side by side, many couples cook amicably together with wonderful results for their families and friends. And in a few cases, men have taken over the bulk of the cooking from the wife who is a reluctant, and sometimes inept, chef.

So, here's to the men! Keep those cards and letters coming—the calls, too.

Odds and Ends

No matter how carefully we plan, there are always the odds and ends.

This brief miscellany has some invaluable recipes. Because they don't fit in the foregoing categories, they are homeless.

I hope you'll take them in.

FANCY CRANBERRIES

Every reader who has tried this has told me she never prepares cranberries any other way now. Or he, either.

1 pound fresh cranberries	6 tablespoons orange marma-
2 cups granulated sugar	lade
1 cup cold water	4 tablespoons lemon juice

Wash and pick the cranberries over. Combine the sugar and water in a saucepan, bring to a boil and cook gently for 5 minutes. Add the cranberries and cook until they have all burst their skins and become rather transparent. Take off the heat, add lemon juice and marmalade. Chill and serve.

Remembrance: Once when I was cooking cranberries, a small seven year old friend of my daughter's watched and listened raptly as the berries softly exploded their skins. "What's that?" she wanted to know. She had never had cranberries except from a can.

I suppose her very nice mamma, having mamma-ed five little girls, didn't have time to pop cranberries.

PEAR CHUTNEY

With chutney now priced up in the caviar class, it's high time to make your own. This one, developed by General Mills, has proved highly satisfactory on several counts: it is sprightly to the taste and does not have to be sterilized-sealed. These amounts make about eight or nine jelly glasses full, those glasses that have plastic tops. It will keep a long time in the refrigerator.

2 pounds green pears, sliced
2 lemons, peeled and sliced
½ pound dark raisins
1½ pounds dark brown sugar
4 garlic cloves, minced
1 large, plus 1 small onion,
   chopped
½ cup candied ginger
2 cans pineapple chunks,
   drained (20 ounce size)

1 pint cider vinegar
¼ cup soy sauce
few dashes Worcestershire
   sauce
1 rounded teaspoon powdered
   cloves
2 teaspoons ground cinnamon
dash of red pepper
Optional: 1½ tablespoons
   mustard seed (I don't use it)

Drain the pineapple. With your swivel potato peeler remove rind from lemons in thin strips and cut into tiny matchsticks. Now, take hold of the suede-like white covering and pull it away from each lemon. Slice, seed the lemons and cut the slices in half.

Combine all the ingredients in a large kettle and cook slowly for about 1 hour until everything is tender. If your batch does not thicken enough, dissolve 1 or 2 tablespoons cornstarch in a little water and stir in at the end. Continue cooking until the sauce is thickened slightly and clear. Pour into clean jars or jelly glasses, cover and store in the refrigerator.

 This is just as good with cold sliced lamb as it is with curry.

HOT TOMATO CHUTNEY

Frani Beach gifted me with a jar of this hot stuff and I thought you all would want it. Excellent with cream cheese as a zingy appetizer and very good alongside cold meats. Hot, hot.

2 pounds ripe tomatoes (5 large ones), peeled, cut-up
1 pint cider vinegar
1 pound raisins
1 large garlic clove
4 cups sugar

½ pound fresh ginger root, peeled and chopped
2 tablespoons (yes!) cayenne pepper
¼ cup salt

Cook tomatoes in vinegar for 15 minutes. Meanwhile, chop raisins and garlic into a paste in the blender or processor, using just enough vinegar to permit the machine to operate.

Add the paste and all remaining ingredients to the tomatoes and simmer until it has the consistency of heavy cream, about 2 hours.

Pour into sterilized jars and seal. This makes 8 jelly glass size jars, 8 ounces each.

SPICY MUSTARD SAUCE

1 cup sour cream
2 tablespoons Dijon mustard
1 tablespoon soy sauce
1 tablespoon Worcestershire sauce

1 teaspoon grated onion
1 garlic clove, crushed
salt and pepper to taste

Mix everything together and serve with cold ham or beef or hamburgers.

Bonus: You can make a quick delicious potato salad using this sauce. Cut ½ cup of it with about 4 tablespoons of cream and toss with dried, freshly-cooked new potatoes. It will want a little more salt. Then add whichever of these you like: a few capers, some basil or tarragon or dill, which was especially good in this dish.

HOT BAKED FRUIT

With almost any brunch menu, this unusual dish gets raves, but it's especially good with sausage and ham and their relatives.

1 package dried prunes (1 pound)	1 can cherry pie filling (1 pound)
1 package dried apricots (11 ounce size)	1½ cups water
1 can pineapple chunks, undrained (13 ounces)	¼ cup dry sherry
	⅓ cup slivered almonds

Just put it all in a big casserole and bake at 350°F for 90 minutes. Serves ten to twelve.

 Sometime when I make this, I'm going to slip in a stick of cinnamon.

PEANUT BUTTER CUPS

One of the girls at my paper made this and found it extremely hard to stop eating. One evening her husband asked her for some candy, and when she came back with it, remarked about how long it had taken her. The reason—she keeps it in the farthest corner of the basement to make temptation difficult. This is so, so easy.

2 sticks margarine, melted	2⅓ cups confectioner's sugar
1¾ cups crushed Graham crackers	2 cups milk chocolate chips (1 package)
1 cup chunky peanut butter	

Mix together the margarine, crumbs, peanut butter and powdered sugar. Pat into a 9 x 13 inch pan.

Melt the chocolate in the top of a double boiler. Spread over the peanut butter layer. Put in the refrigerator to cool and set, but don't let it harden or it will be difficult to cut. Check in about 15 minutes then, gauge your time to cut into squares when it is firm but not hard.

Then—hide it!

SISTER ALICE'S SWEET PICKLES

Have your own distinctive pickles without the work.

1 pint sliced hamburger dill pickles, commercial	1 cup white sugar
¼ cup tarragon vinegar	1 teaspoon mustard seed
	1 teaspoon celery seed

Drain and wash the pickles. Dry on paper towels.

In a saucepan, combine vinegar and sugar. Heat, then add seasonings. Put the dried pickles back in the jar, pour over the hot vinaigrette and allow to stand.

Chill and serve. These are extra good with grilled cheese sandwiches.

RED RASPBERRY SAUCE

In a positive fit of nostalgia for a long ago night in a European opera house, I made this one day just for myself! On that memorable night I recall coming down the sweep of marble stairs and smelling the most heady, sweet aroma. It was a sauce like this, kept hot in chafing dishes and served over vanilla ice cream during the intermission. It was either Vienna or Munich. Can't remember.

1 package frozen red raspberries (10 ounce size)
⅓ cup sugar
1 tablespoon, plus 1 teaspoon
  cornstarch

1 tablespoon lemon juice
1 tablespoon cognac

Thaw the berries slightly then put in a saucepan with the sugar. Meanwhile, dissolve the cornstarch in a few tablespoons of the cold raspberry juice.

Bring the berries and sugar to a boil, then force through a fine sieve. Put the strained liquid back in the saucepan, add the dissolved cornstarch and cook gently, stirring, until the sauce thickens and looks clear. When it has cooled somewhat, stir in the lemon juice and cognac.

Serve hot or cold over ice cream.

 If you make this with fresh berries, you may not need as much cornstarch. Go gently. This is the sauce you use for Peche Melba. Put a fresh peach half over the ice cream, then ladle the raspberry sauce over.

SWEET AND SOUR SAUCE

½ cup firmly packed brown
  sugar
3 tablespoons cornstarch

1 cup pineapple juice
3 tablespoons cider vinegar
3 tablespoons soy sauce

Put everything in a small saucepan and cook, stirring constantly until the sauce thickens and clears. Cook for one more minute, then serve over leftover fowl.

CREAMY GRAVY

2 tablespoons chopped green
  onions
3 tablespoons butter or margarine
¼ cup flour

1½ cups chicken broth
½ cup light cream
1 tablespoon chopped parsley
salt and pepper to taste

Sauté onions gently in butter in a medium saucepan. Stir in flour, mix well, then add the chicken broth. Cook over low heat until the sauce thickens. Add cream and parsley and simmer just 3 minutes. Taste for seasoning and serve over leftover fowl.

A Bouquet for You

No woman in the world is as interested, curious, or inventive in her home cooking as an American woman.

Can you imagine a Frenchwoman in Normandy trying a recipe for American chili? She doesn't even try the cuisine of southern France, for her cooking is regional. But you cook Northern and Southern French with the same aplomb as you cook all the regions of the States.

Do you suppose many ladies in China have ever made a lemon meringue pie? I doubt it. Yet you have acquired a wok, and have learned to stir fry with a light hand.

Does a Spanish signora make sauerkraut, or a German hausfrau serve a paella? Not a chance. But you do.

A great chef on a splendid transatlantic liner once told me he liked to give cooking demonstrations to Americans much more than to the French passengers. "The Americans want to learn," he said. "Frenchwomen look down their noses and announce that the way I'm doing it isn't the way they do it."

This eclectic enthusiasm of American women (and men) in their kitchens is always increasing and has occasioned many ethnic cook books, lots of special equipment and an easy familiarity with table wines. It has given your families more variety in menu than ever before.

It seems to me that it all began after World War II—when the men came home from the European theatre particularly.

In spite of the widespread propaganda, well nurtured by the films, that all they wanted was apple pie, many soldiers had actually expanded their tastes while abroad. Many had learned to drink wine with food. Certainly they brought back a liking for the simple green salad, an alternative to the composed or gelatin salads we customarily served.

In Italy, they discovered the delights of pasta a hundred ways. In Paris, on leave, they savored cooking such as they had never experienced. While it took some years to become wide-spread here, the trend, I do believe, began then.

Not much culinary inspiration came out of England, but not a great deal has happened since either. The British tend to like things the way they are. I recall, a few years ago, taking the fast ferry out of Le Havre to the south of England. A group of British traveling together kept looking across the water to the visible coast with obvious pleasure.

I asked one lady if she'd be glad to be home again. After a gala weekend in Paris, she could only remark that she couldn't wait to get home, put the kettle on and have a proper cup of tea.

In that same boat, you would have been trying to figure out what was in that shellfish gratin—Pernod, perhaps?

Keep up the good work.

Index